THE MASTERY CODE

Self-Mastery • Money-Mastery • Purpose

LLEWELLYN DEVEREAUX

THE MASTERY CODE

The Mastery Code
Self-Mastery • Money-Mastery • Purpose

ISBN: 978-0-620-86752-8

This paperback first edition published in 2020
Second Reprint 18 June 2020

First published in Cape Town in 2020 by
Llewellyn Devereaux
10 Center Road
Morningside
Sandton
2057

Typeset in Durban, South Africa
Printed in South Africa

Acknowledgements:

Thank you to everyone who has helped me on my journey and been a part of it, I have tremendous gratitude for you all.

To my mom and dad, Margaret and George, this is for you!

"The man who succeeds above his fellows is the one who early in life, clearly discerns his object, and towards that object, habitually directs his powers. Even genius itself is but fine observation strengthened by fixity of purpose. Every man who observes vigilantly and resolves steadfastly grows unconsciously into genius."

- Edward Bulwer-Lytton

This is my gift to you, the reader, who wants to set their own new standard in the world from within and I hope this book benefits not only you but everyone you grow to touch through your own authentic expression of who you are. I hope that you grow powerful, wealthy and full of purpose radiating with happiness as a light to everyone you come into contact with!

Nosce te Ipsum

TABLE OF CONTENTS

PART ONE - UNLEARNING

PART TWO - LEARNING

PART THREE -RE-LEARNING

THE MASTERY CODE

Self-Mastery • Money-Mastery • Purpose

PART ONE

UNLEARNING

Chapter 1

GENESIS

we are automatically affected by our environment before we can become aware of it.

I

Over the years, I have come to the realization that something very peculiar was done to us. When I say "done to us", I don't mean in a conspiracy theorist kind of way, but in a sense that you gave no consent or active participation in it until you grow up and start asking yourself some serious questions about life.

Eventually, you are able to look at society with observant eyes and really start looking at it for what it really is, versus looking at it for what you wish it could be.

When you start doing this, you move into a powerful new mental position of being able to call a spade a spade. No more distracting, silly terms such as "I am using this superbly engineered piece of metal to more easily move large lumps of sand from one spot to another."

We, as a species, have come to over-complicate almost every plight we experience. We do this to try and feel better. Somehow, by assigning some scary sounding name to the situation, we not only identify it when we see it but also come to admire it. Sadly, we have become extremely good at admiring problems.

It doesn't take any special awareness to be able to look at society and make a call on what is apparent; some of us have lost focus of the truth. Together, in this book, we will refocus ourselves and work towards a better life.

The process and complexity of life fascinate me with its vastness. Here we all are, nearly eight billion human beings, all of whom should be asking the same eternal question, where did we come from, and where are we going? Some of us have lost so much focus that we have forgotten that we should be asking the question.

Each of us come into existence with no idea we are even alive for the first few years of life, and in those years all we're doing is trying to absorb as much as we can from this new experience. Some of us are born into beautiful homes with parents that love them and have prepared for their arrival. In contrast, the majority of people are born into uncongenial circumstances and remain in a state of unawareness of their full potential.

In the Steve Jobs movie, there is a line by John Sculley who asks Steve (who was given away at birth), why orphaned children choose to look at what happened to them as being rejected versus being chosen? Jobs replied with: "It's all about control; what could a one-day-old baby have done that was so bad that he had to be given away?"

Jobs further went on to say that it's all about control to him, and when you realize how little of it you have, you want to keep it, and most people aren't even aware of this.

At birth we are just thrown into an environment that we can't fathom, escape or have control over; what makes it worse is that we can't even communicate until we have absorbed the language of our environment. So, we are automatically affected by our environment before we can become aware of it.

The question however, is, does one ever become aware of it? If a person was born into a prison and was never made aware of this, does that person just accept that this is life? This was the question that Plato asked in his cave analysis.

(I encourage you to YouTube Plato's Allegory of the cave).

This is the case of Neo in the movie The Matrix. He was not aware he was in the Matrix until he was unplugged. And even then, his mind was against the truth Morpheus was trying to relay to him.

This is the situation most of society finds themselves in. This book is a red pill of sorts. This book is not designed to indoctrinate you into my way of thinking or any way of thinking for that matter. This book is designed to make you look at yourself and shine a light on who you really are, whatever you find that to be.

Only when the student is ready will the master appear.

You will only get from this book what you are ready to receive. This book cannot be a manual, only a ladder. I can only give you the tools, share my experiences and the wisdom I have gained from Masters before me. Only you can help yourself by assuming full responsibility and taking action from wherever you find yourself in your life.

Each person must discover who they are. Only when you seek the answers can they be revealed to you, and this requires you to be open to the beautiful possibilities that are awaiting you on this journey.

Everything in your life has led you to this point where you find yourself reading this book, and it was perfectly orchestrated for this to happen to you, and for you right now wherever you are.

So, take this as a profound and critical moment in your life, and it will be so. The journey of self-discovery is not an easy one but will be the most beneficial thing for you to do.

It will not only benefit you but everyone around you.

You have a right to be here; you have a right to have everything you want, you have a right to do every good thing you want to do, with anyone you wish to do it with, provided that you obviously don't harm someone else.

You have a right to have a good time.

You matter and what you do matters, even though you've believed everything contrary to this truth.

The world is filled with conspiracies; conspiracies that intentionally try to prevent you from seeing the truth.

My deepest hope is that you discover who you are, find your gifts and unlock the courage that is awaiting you.

I hope that courage will grant you the fire you need to carve out your own path in life that will lead you serendipitously to everything you've ever wanted. Enjoy the ride and be manifested.

Chapter 2

SOCIETY

Humanity has never been more distracted.

"We have created society and that society has conditioned us."
- Jiddu Krishnamurti

II

The year as I am writing this is 2018. As I look outside my balcony door looking at the new affluent neighbourhood I currently reside in; I can't help but think about how differently each person alive today experiences what we call reality.

Life is different for all of us. I look out at the world and ponder about what it must feel like to be everyone as a collective, all at the same time. To be able to know and feel what everyone thinks, and how they choose to perceive life, how life differs from the viewpoint of each country and language.

These questions fascinate me. I have always worked on seeing things from another's point of view. I truly value the ability to get out of myself and all my needs and somewhat insert my consciousness into the circumstances of others. It becomes a powerful learning experience when you can let go of your own ego from time to time and simply marvel at life.

I have had the privilege of watching life become more digital as the years have passed. I watched the world go from an analogue to a more digital world and witnessed the rise of social media and the internet as a whole new industry.

Humanity has never been more distracted. Everything and everyone is fighting for your attention; from brands to politics to the news. It is disturbing to note how little time we now have to ourselves with how much time we spend looking at marketing materials and the lives of others online.

Marketers have now claimed that the average human attention span is now the lowest it has ever been at 8 seconds versus what it was in 2000 at 12 seconds. Research has found that this rate is expected to decrease annually. All it takes for you to see this is to go to a restaurant or public place without your phone, order a coffee or a drink and just watch people. It will blow your mind.

Even more frightening is the apparent increase of depression, mental health issues as well as suicides that plague humanity. I am no expert in these matters, and so I won't go into it because these things have a way of getting overly technical and tragically even more glamorised. My heart is with the victims and their families.

We have an extremely unhappy society that is constantly plagued by ideas of what their lives should be, struggling to deal with the daily variance of their lives not being close to the image social media has created in their minds.

It doesn't take an expert to see that if you believe that everyone's lives are significantly better than your own, that will in-turn make you unhappy. I wouldn't diagnose it as depression lest I upset the experts, but a lot of what we see just requires common sense to make a call on the evidence.

Too many people find everyone else far more interesting than themselves and so they dedicate all of their time and energy towards these people who they don't really know or who don't really exist anyway. Everyone is quick to project a perfect image of themselves online yet struggle to deal with reality. As a result of this, many turn to drugs, alcohol and other substances to cope. I have recently concluded that the drugs, alcohol and other substances are not the actual addiction; the need to escape reality is.

I see a highly dependent society, one that takes too much from the planet and gives back very little or nothing.

It definitely has never been in the best interest of any power structure in society to have citizens that are capable of critical thinking and have an independent mindset. What would happen to all the governments, churches and many organisations when their people/members realise that they really don't need to be a part of any of those orders, who will pay the rent, the taxes etc.?

We are a mentally enslaved population that has been sold a fake identity of ourselves that is far removed from our true core. We put up with conditions simply because we are afraid of the shame that can come from standing up for ourselves. People stay in jobs that are destroying their health and happiness all in the name of being employed and having an income. People remain in relationships that are doing nothing but hurting them all because of a fear of being alone; people don't have the ability to be alone anymore.

Many people also choose to be around people that never uplift or better them in any way simply because of some warped sense of loyalty. Misery is easy because happiness takes effort and society is geared today to profit off of the misfortunes of people.

It was Earl Nightingale who said that the greatest plague in society today is not fear but conformity.

People are not playing follow the leader, but more playing follow the follower. People, doing things for the sake of doing them because everybody else is doing it regardless of whether they fit them or not. People seldom bother asking why.

It is as if the only way people can identify themselves in this world is via a mould that has been or is being lived by someone else.

At some point, you have to be able to stop being so nice to yourself, put yourself on trial and ask yourself some really important questions even though you might not be happy about the answers.

When last did you ask yourself if you were happy about a situation in your life and if not, come up with solutions for it instead of coming up with excuses for why you should remain in it because that is the way other people have done it.

It's almost as if this life is something that must be endured and survived in the promise of a better afterlife provided we behave and follow a particular way of living here on Earth today. We have subscribed to unhappiness and anxiety and have adopted that belief system, and that is exactly what we get for it is done unto you as you believe.

What I've learnt, however, is that regardless of how digital the world can become, there is no substitute for reality.

Chapter 3

CIRCUMSTANCES

The trees need the winter drought and cold as much as they need the summer rains.

"People are anxious to improve their circumstances but are unwilling to improve themselves. They therefore remain bound."
- James Allen

III

In the previous chapter, I said that what we have done is subscribe to life being a constant struggle. We have accepted unhappiness and anxiety. Notice how I use the word "subscribe". The dictionary says, "subscribe" means to arrange, to receive something or to express or feel agreement with an idea or proposal.

There is a universal law (more on this later) called The Law of Rhythm, which states that the energy in the universe is like a pendulum. Whenever something swings to the right, it must swing to the left. Everything in existence is involved in a dance, swaying, flowing and changing, just like the different seasons. Nothing is ever static and staying in one constant state.

The trees need the winter drought and cold as much as they need the summer rains. If we can accept this in nature, why do we not accept this in our own lives?

We are taught to treat adverse circumstances as something we should be surprised by, and should thus, always be in a state of preparing for them when they aren't apparent. We are taught to live life in defence mode.

What computer gaming taught me about life is that you will never progress to the next stage if you can't defeat the level you're currently on. What it also taught me was that the game is not supposed to get easier! The game is there; life is there to test and develop my skills and make me better.

Life was never designed to get easier just because you desperately wish it to be so, but you are designed to rise above and evolve from certain conditions in your life.

You are not a slave to the conditions of your life.

You can only go higher when you can defeat your current level. As a result of missing this wisdom, many people go through life with the same struggles in finances, relationships and other areas. The cliché saying: "What you resist, persists" I wish someone had taught this to me earlier on in my life or at school. This simply means that the lessons in life we refuse to confront and improve upon will keep repeating themselves as circumstances in our lives. In other words, you will suffer the same heartbreak from different people if you don't become aware of the root cause of it and face it internally for what it is.

What if I were to propose an idea that stipulates that we chose the circumstances required for our own individual evolution and thus maybe even waited for them to be so. We waited for the alignment to this time, demanded that we be brought here with our own set of unique gifting, and we then orchestrated a chain reaction of events that resulted in us appearing as a result of a sexual encounter of our parents.

Sure this might be rather a drastic and idealistic point of view, but this viewpoint basically says that you chose the conditions of your life instead of it being the choice of some higher power, or that you randomly just appeared here and must now figure this life thing out for yourself somehow leaving you with a feeling of helplessness.

Maybe some readers might be asking themselves: "If I chose the circumstances, why didn't I choose better circumstances; why would I have chosen to be born into the situation I was born into? "

I can totally understand that line of questioning, and I certainly don't have the answers for such a question, but my viewpoint gives you a certain level of progressive power towards your life versus a regressive view that does nothing but cause you to play the blame game.

Gaming also taught me that life will only dish out to you according to the measure of that which we can handle and only promotes you when you can go beyond that. I definitely would not be able to handle someone else's problems, and they vice versa could not handle mine.

We look at people's lives and covet them, but we don't see what they are secretly battling with when they are alone at night in their beds. People only project what they want to show you. People make the mistake of assuming that what is projected is what a person experiences twenty-four-seven.

I have been through things in making my companies successful that I didn't even know I could overcome. During the process I never let people in unless they were close to me and could offer some support; what I've learnt however is that life will promote you to the extent of your ability to handle conflict and your ability to make sacrifices in order to go higher. Upward evolution demands downward elimination because you can't occupy two opposing states of being simultaneously. So when you see a person whose life you think is perfect because they appear successful or perfect, also know that there is a heavy price that had to be paid; there is no something for nothing in the universe. Another universal law called "The law of cause and effect" talks on this.

Most people struggle with money, but I see that is the conversation that they choose to engage in the least. Why? Simply because of fear, and so we signed an invisible contract with each other to glorify finances being a problem because so many people are in the same sinking boat. It's funny how we can normalize chaos when it is popular to the group at large.

But have you ever asked for help, or went out seeking financial education for your financial situation? If the answer is no, then you understand why you struggle with finances and will continue to do so. And if you have received sound financial education and are still struggling, then it is safe to be honest with yourself and investigate why the knowledge you received, you didn't apply.

We need to deal with the world the way it really is, and it really is on you to assume full responsibility for your life. Be willing to learn the things that other people aren't. Be willing to pay to learn and not wait for someone else to pay in order for you to learn, this approach to life instils autonomy, and that autonomy automatically grants you power.

Life isn't easy or hard; it just is. I do not think there is a deity up there somewhere only helping a few or a counter deity somewhere below that is responsible for suffering that we ought to blame. I accept that you might believe that to be the case and if that is your choice then that is your choice, and maybe the things I am saying here could add to what you already know or believe and act to benefit you in some way.

You will notice as you read on that I choose and embody a state of mind that is beneficial to me and not one that is detrimental to me. I think that regardless of what you believe in, you can also choose to filter out that which is detrimental and then add to that, only what is beneficial to you.

I choose to think that everything responds to what we believe it to be; that we experience what we focus on, and all reality mirrors us. What we each experience in the world is the outcome of our idea about it. We do this consciously or unconsciously by projecting an intention with our actions into life. Therefore circumstances are there to reveal man to himself.

I have come to see that life is not about it being some difficult thing to deal with, but we have just been poorly educated on it, and that is why we suffer (more in the next chapter).

We have been intentionally educated with restrictions and are thus inadequately prepared to deal with life, and this is why we suffer; we never grow into the full truth of this. We can agree that chess is just a game, but if you don't learn the rules of it, you will continue to be beaten and not understand why.

All circumstances are there to make you better, so don't shy away from them, avoid them or believe that they are special and unique to you. Everyone must face their own life, and playing the victim is what most of the population does. This book aims to teach you how to adopt a powerful and progressive belief system at your core which allows you to understand that circumstances are normal and a part of life in such a way that they empower you. I want you to begin walking through life, knowing you have a right to be here with your head held high. Not as someone holy or pious, but just as someone who understands this as a concept.

Chapter 4

PROGRAMMING/ BELIEF SYSTEM

birds born in a cage think flying is an illness.

"You are today the result of your thoughts of yesterday, and the many yesterdays' preceding it. You are forming today the mould for what you will be in the years to come."
- Robert Collier

IV

Everything we experience is a result of our personal subscription to it.

In the previous chapter, I eluded to the concept of programming.

Whether we like to admit it or not, we are a product of the influences we've allowed into our lives. The saying "show me your friends and I'll show you who you are" is one of the most underrated phrases ever said because I feel it doesn't fully capture the message that it is trying to convey.

Your environment has such a powerful influence on you but not because of the things that you're aware of, but because of the things you become that you didn't even know you allowed into your life.

Think about it...
Before the age of reason; your language, accent, religion, your schooling, political views, sports team, view of money, view on

relationships, behaviour and many other traits you adopted were shaped by your parents or any other guardian who had custody over you.

This means who you start off as in this world is a derivative of everything you encounter in aggregate.

People who come from loving families have a higher propensity to want to re-create that in their own lives because that's what they know. Similarly, people who come from homes that are absent of love will struggle to emulate that all simply because it is something new they need to desire, learn and implement. It is almost like having to learn a whole new language you might not know you needed to learn.

Psychologists have taken it further by saying that everything you experience by age eight sticks to your personality for life. The old Jesuit maxim proves true: "Give me the child for the first seven years, and I'll give you the man."

They say birds born in a cage think flying is an illness.

To understand the severity of this saying, just imagine having an identical twin brother or sister who gets kidnapped at birth and ends up living with people in poverty while you grow up in a wealthy family. Then imagine meeting up with them again 20 years later. How different do you think things will be? Play on that for some time.

We are all living walking results of our programming. If you grew up poor, chances are, you will stay there and vice versa, if you come from a wealthy family, chances are you will stay there all because of programming.

95% of your thinking is made up of your thinking from the previous day. Only 5% of your daily thinking is conscious and new (more on this later). This means that 95% of who you are today, you were yesterday and most probably in the days preceding that. This is then further solidified and crystallizes the longer you tend to stay in that environment around the same influences.

I also once came across a concept in neuroscience called "mirror neurons" which is the parts of the brain that facilitate imitation. This is what causes babies to move how they move when they try to imitate those around them who dance or do some other form of repetitive movement. What "mirror neurons" do is get us to adapt as quickly as we can to the environment around us; this is programmed into the human design.

The shows you watch, the pages you follow, the radio shows you listen to, the people you surround yourself with and the information you consume all sum up your character and those combined with your habits are creating your future where you are right now.

If you hate where you are in life right now, know that that is primarily due to your programming. Your struggles in life are not because some devil out there is out to attack you, or some higher power is punishing you. These problems exist because your programming in that area of your life doesn't support the conclusion you hold in your mind. If you were learning to drive a manual car and were struggling with the clutch control; there isn't anything wrong with the car, you just haven't acquired the program to drive a car. With enough practice, you will find that you can not only drive that car but any manual car afterwards. Was the car the issue? No. The issue was your programming.

The same can be said about life, and I will repeat what I said before; where you struggle in your life is a result of programs that you have running subconsciously that don't support the conclusion you are desperate to achieve, and nobody will tell you this. We're all going through life putting up a front in public with beautiful smiles while we suffer in private.

Nobody taught us about relationships, about the tax system, dealing with fame and influence, about making money, contracts, dealing with people, investing, saving, conflict, heartbreak, happiness, how to get rich, purpose and about all the issues that we deal with on a daily basis. If you doubt this concept, ask yourself when last you used Pythagoras to deal with an issue of life?

We also tend to think that having some college or university education automatically gives you an intricate understanding of life. What makes this even scarier is that most people stop learning after they graduate, and if they do learn something, it is only to get themselves into a higher income bracket.

A degree only shows a willingness to learn, but it isn't learning. You also see this with how little of your degree or qualification you use in the real world unless you studied something practical that you apply on a daily basis.

I came to the shocking reality that after almost 17 years of school and tertiary education, we know close to nothing about the life we deal with on a daily basis going forward. It's a scary thing to realize and then to admit that we were not taught anything. We were given the illusion of education. When you look at the results people get in life, it appears only a select few got a real or a hidden education, and now everyone is in awe of them.

This hit me and made me realize that I had to understand why this is so. This got me asking questions instead of having pride in it. Asking a question makes you a fool for 5 seconds, and this is better than being a fool your whole life.

The truth I am conveying might be a little painful to swallow. You are where you are today because of all that you have been exposed to and accepted. Where you struggle in life is not because of what you know but because of what you don't know. The system has intentionally kept the truth from you, in order to profit off of your misfortunes. Your programming has been sabotaged and only when you know better, can you then do better, but until then, your results will continue to be the very same results you do not want.

Just because you are alive, and breathing does not mean you're automatically qualified to deal with life, especially at the level you wish to experience it. Just because you have a degree doesn't mean you are qualified in the issues of life.

Right now, I want you to say something out loud to yourself: "I KNOW NOTHING!"

Now repeat it louder.

Admitting you know nothing is the beginning of wisdom. You think you know something but the results you are getting versus the results you wish to be getting in life are incongruent because I'm assuming you didn't buy this book to read it as a bedtime story but to make something profound of your life.

The bridge between where you are now and where you wish to be in terms of results is called "a new and progressive mindset ", and the steps you must take to get you there require you to adopt a new way of thinking before you can master a new way of being.

You become powerful when you can decide where you want to be or what you want out of life and you understand that in order to get there, you are going to have to adopt a new way of thinking followed by a symmetrical set of new actions. It is not easy, but it is possible as this requires you to practice enough consistency in order to breach the beginner phase of anything new. The people who move themselves are the people who move the world. Once one has discovered the concept of programming, you can effectively program yourself and apply the necessary actions and patience and achieve the result. This makes most events in life we have control over somewhat predictable.

There is nothing magical or miraculous about this concept; it is just that nobody has taught this to you until now.

Realize that you have been intentionally mis-educated, that your life today is the result of the programming which you have unknowingly subscribed to in the past, and that your life in the future will be determined by the programming that you choose to subscribe to today going forward.

Chapter 5

HUMAN NATURE

most people you encounter, walk around with masks on

"You take people, you put them on a journey, you give them peril, you find out who they really are."
- Joss Whedon

V

If there is one area, I can say I've learnt some hard lessons in, it has to be here; dealing with our fellow human beings. Human beings have been the source of my greatest pleasure, as well as my greatest pain. I am grateful that I chose a line of life that forced me to not only realise myself, but forced me to see others for what they truly are in my life during my 20s. A lot of people, however, aren't as fortunate, and this is why I want to dedicate a full chapter to this topic.

"No man or woman is an island" is another old and often overused saying. It's a cliche, and it is one simply because it is so completely true! I cannot sit here and say that I don't need people at all because I am where I am today because of every single human being that has contributed to my life. I now try to deal with as few human beings as possible. Sometimes I think human beings are tiring, that is when I think cats are better.

Society is wired in such a way that most people you encounter, walk around with masks on hiding private battles and many other "issues".

You don't discover these issues of theirs until you get too close.

Social media has not made this easier. People have immense pressure to project the best parts about themselves, and this has created a "mist" effect that makes many of us believe that everyone's lives are significantly more perfect than our own. So, we go into life, expecting this online perfection of them only to be disappointed upon encountering the reality behind the mist.

I, by no means have figured it all out, but I am writing now from the perspective of having lost close to everything I once knew in the pursuit of my dreams. This loss forced me to have to rebuild myself completely. This rebuild touched every aspect of my life and allowed me a clear view into the lives of people surrounding me at the time. There is so much to be gained when you don't have to pretend in this life. It was only when I had very little to pretend with, that I began to pierce through the illusion people put up as their "mist".

At our core, we have boundless potential. As a species, I think we are compassionate, we are loving, and we don't wish harm upon others; but things change when we are thrust into an arena of life where we are forced to operate from a perspective of lack that assumes that the pie keeps getting smaller and smaller.

While competition drives much progress, it has been responsible for bringing out the worst in human beings. The concept of you winning, meaning someone else losing, is the very thing that drives us to the dark side. Only once a person can ascend from the perspective of lack into the perspective of abundance can one truly start to appreciate themselves as well as their fellow human beings and creation in general. Without the perspective of abundance, it is difficult to truly be happy for other people, especially when they are doing better than you.

It is simple; as long as a person is in survival mode, everything they do, has themselves at the centre, regardless of who or what they have to hurt to achieve their objectives. This all stems from fear-based thinking.

Napoleon Hill highlights the fear of criticism as one of the six major fears human beings deal with. This fear does something very sinister to the individual; it exacerbates suffering at the hand of people close to us in the name of some warped sense of loyalty to history, traditions, emotional or family ties. Pain is temporary, but sustained suffering is your choice!

Let me be blunt and make this as clear as possible for you:

For as long as you put other people's needs above your own at the expense of yourself, your resources and your peace, you will continue to suffer.

Someone who continues to let you suffer at their hands intentionally does not have your best interests at heart; they are not for you!

These people only want you for what you can provide them.

You owe it to yourself to break away because only then can your progress begin!

The only people that get mad at you for having boundaries are the people that benefit from you having none. I have come to see that we have become a society that glorifies suffering. I know adversity and struggle are a part of life and something that comes easy isn't worth having, but I have everything against unnecessary or self-inflicted suffering over time. The desert is only a temporary phase and not a permanent one.

You have a right to be happy, you have a right to enjoy your life, and you have a right to choose how your life will turn out. The fear of criticism stops people from making decisions that benefit them. This fear gets worse at lower income levels and so do its effects.

Some people will be reading this now thinking that it's not easy to just apply a new philosophy and run with it and I understand, but I'm also not here to waste words and lie to you because I am interested in your progress and not your failure. No matter how strong you think you are, you will eventually get tired if you carry too many parasites.

I believe, and I say it often, that at our core we are good, and we want to help others; the thing that gets most of us is that we want to help others from an empty cup. The aim of this book is not for you to stay where you are, but for you to rise up in your power so that you can become more, have more and then be able to help the people you wish to help. You can't provide effective and lasting help if every time you help, you cut large parts of yourself away in the process.

People want to help people, but they help them from a place of weakness. You want to be able to help people from a cup that is running over because that will feed you rather than make you feel bad about feeding others. You never want to be in a position where you regret helping others.

I used to be the kind of person that instantly saw the good in people. I saw their potential and celebrated it with them. I began to see this as a gift. This gift gave me great pleasure when people who were around me started to want to create and express themselves more. It was almost as if my journey had unconsciously given people the grounds to express themselves freely. I guess people are afraid to talk to other people about the beautiful things that they think about in solitude. This gift, however, can be destructive if you do not also look after yourself.

The point I'm trying to make is that I was blind at first to the consequences of other people taking advantage of my gift to see the best in them. Now I am extremely selective with who I allow into my space and who gets to feed off of me. I made the mistake of allowing everyone the reigns to feed off of me, and that cost me years.

Most people are afraid and extremely insecure about who they are. So, when they see you as a shining positive light, they naturally will be drawn to you, especially if their reality is in a constant state of darkness. If you've seen how moths are drawn to light; you will see that nature has already given this lesson and this you must be aware of as you start to peel off the limitations that have been holding you back.

Vet every single person in your life, make sure that people are feeding you as much as you are feeding them. Learn to say no and stop betraying yourself, if you don't want to do or go somewhere, don't feel bad when you refuse. You don't need to apologise for your honesty, those who have an issue with it need to evolve.

Self-betrayal becomes a habit that goes unnoticed the more you practice it. Self-love is much talked about in success literature, but pop culture has turned it into a "kumbaya" song, stripped of any real meaning.

You cannot make everyone happy, and even attempting that is a losing formula from the get-go. It is better to start by making yourself happy.

I am by no means saying that you should make yourself happy by hurting others, but if you being happy means others are hurt, then you're dealing with a dysfunctional relationship.

There will be some who will be unhappy with the decisions you make, and that's something you must be ok with if you want to be happy. If your decisions hurt people, check your actions and then check those people.

Bishop TD Jakes classifies the three kinds of people in your life:

Confidants: The people that are for you.

Regardless of what you're about, these people feel such a deep connection to you that they cannot leave, nor can you leave them. It's almost as if your destinies are intertwined. These are at most two or three people in your life. If you have these in your life; consider yourself blessed.

Constituents: The people that are for what you are for.

These people will be willing to sit with you so long as you share the same interests, destinations and ideas. As soon as you change what you are for, expect them to change their presence in your life. These people will also leave you as soon as they get a better deal or quicker one.

I've seen a lot of people get upset about friends and loved ones who walked out on them as soon as they changed jobs or started pursuing their dreams. Remember, not everyone is in your life for your journey; it is your journey, and you cannot expect everyone to come with you, the door is for you to walk through. Most are not qualified or built to handle it; you will find, however, that all the people that walk out of your life because of you pursuing you, did you a favour.

Most of our friendships are in this category; sadly, the only way to know who your true friends are is to see who sticks around when you go through dark times. Only then will you know who your confidants are and who your constituents are, but these tend to feel the same in the interim until trials happen in your life.

Comrades: The people that form a friendship with you based on a common enemy or common dislike, or common momentary objective that goes against yours.

As soon as the enemy, dislike or objective is met or dealt with, the friendship itself dissolves because they were not built on solid grounds but common momentary objectives.

The whole conversation on people is an extensive one that probably requires an entire book, but the aim is for you to rate and vet the people that are in your life. You are the sum total of the five people you spend most of your time around, and this is something that I used to think was bogus, but these words deserve to be on everyone's bathroom mirror.

It is important that you understand that you must learn to help yourself first before you can effectively help other people. You must be aware that most people are unhappy because misery is easy because it is the default, and happiness takes constant effort, but this doesn't have to be your reality. You must learn to protect your peace and your energy because nobody will do it for you. It is on you to assume 100% responsibility for your life and the people you choose to be around. Be extremely selective with the people you allow in your inner circle and have extremely high standards that you feel unapologetic about, only then will you become who you are truly meant to be.

Be around people that make you feel good about yourself, especially when you know you're destined for greatness. I used to be around people who I didn't even know hated me, but they hated me because I was focused and energetic. They tried to make me feel bad about it. I have learnt that being around these kinds of people will dim your light in the long run; you will feel bad for shining your light; these are not your people!

Remember that self-mastery and the expression of your individuality is initially a lonely journey. Nobody can tell you what goes on in between the person you are and the person you wish to become; it's binary. Either you are going to make it out the other side or you won't.

One last thing I have to say before we wrap up this chapter: let go of unproductive people in your life. This definitely will prove to be easier said than done, but this will single-handedly be the first major move in the direction of the identification and acceptance of your own unique rhythm. These unproductive people you enjoy being around are the very same ones that make progress seem like a foreign concept to you, and that is why it keeps eluding you. These people can be in the form of family, lovers as well as friends.

Letting go might prove to be drastic for some but what you can do is limit your time with these people once you become aware of them - at least up until some time has passed and you happen to be in momentum with everything that you want to accomplish.

Chapter 6

GRATIFICATION

Once upon a time, there were three little pigs...

"Incessantly demanding that I am given some 'thing' today may very well destroy the role that it was going to play in my life tomorrow."
- Craig D. Lounsbrough

VI

The three little pigs is a fable that everyone should know. Most of us think we have learnt the lesson it offers, but I have uncovered a deeper wisdom in it. Let us revisit the story.

The story goes like this:

Once upon a time, there were three little pigs who lived with their mother in the woods, the pigs were of age, and the mother decided that they now had to leave home and go make their own fortunes. Before they left, however, the mom gave them one piece of advice: "Whatever you do, do it the best way that you can because that's the way to get along in the world." The little pigs went off to seek their fortunes and build their houses.

The first one was lazy, he didn't want to work too hard on the house and wanted to get this done as quickly as possible, so he built his house out of straw which was the easiest thing to do. The second pig worked a little bit harder than the first, but he was somewhat lazy too, so he built his house out of sticks. They both were done fairly quickly and played the whole day.

The third pig worked hard and laboured all day to build his house with bricks. The other two laughed at their brother, the third pig because he couldn't play with them all day, but he didn't let that hinder him, and he eventually finished.

There was a wolf that walked past the lane where they lived, and he smelled the first pig inside his straw house and thought the pig would be quite a treat to eat. He went over to the door, and he said, "Let me in, let me in, little pig or I'll huff, and I'll puff, and I'll blow your house in!"

"Not by the hair of my chinny chin chin", said the little pig. But of course, the wolf did blow the house down, but luckily the pig managed to escape to his brother's house, made with sticks.

The wolf continued down the lane, and he passed by the second house made of sticks, and he saw the house, and again he smelled the pigs inside, and his mouth began to water as he thought about the fine dinner they would make.

So he knocked on the door and said: "Let me in, Let me in, little pigs or I'll huff, and I'll puff, and I'll blow your house down!"

"Not by the hair of my chinny chin chin", echoed the little pigs. So he huffed, and he puffed, and he blew the house down! The wolf was greedy, and he tried to catch both pigs at once, but he was too greedy and got neither! His big jaws clamped down on nothing, but air and the two little pigs scrambled away as fast as their little hooves would carry them.

The wolf chased them down the lane, and he almost caught them, but they made it to the brick house and slammed the door closed before the wolf could catch them.

The three little pigs were very frightened; they knew the wolf wanted to eat them, and that was very, very true. The wolf hadn't eaten all day, and he had worked up a massive appetite chasing the pigs around, and now he could smell all three of them inside, and he knew that the three little pigs would make a lovely feast.

So the wolf knocked on the door once again and said: "Let me in, let me in" cried the wolf, "Or I'll huff, and I'll puff till I blow your house in!"

"Not by the hair of my chinny chin chin" chimed the pigs together.

Well, the wolf huffed and puffed, but he could not blow down that brick house. But the wolf was a sly old wolf, and he climbed up on the roof to look for a way into the brick house.
The little pigs saw the wolf climb up on the roof and lit a roaring fire in the fireplace and placed on it a large kettle of water.

When the wolf finally found the hole in the chimney, he crawled down and KERSPLASH right into that kettle of water, and that was the end of their troubles with the big bad wolf.

The day after the mother pig came and saw the little pigs and she heard the story and was glad that one of her little pigs heeded her words that said: "Whatever you do, do it the best way that you can because that's the way to get along in the world."

The focused, proud determination and delayed gratification of the third pig, is what saved all their lives.

The story itself is what we've always known the story to be, but I figured it would make a great opening to the topic of delayed gratification.

Everyone has a choice to make in life; you are either going to adapt your life for short term gains or adapt your life for long term gains.

The word gratification, according to the dictionary, means to derive pleasure, especially when gained from the satisfaction of a desire. This can be divided up into instant gratification and delayed gratification.

INSTANT / IMMEDIATE GRATIFICATION.

This is the term that refers to the temptation and resulting tendency to forgo a future benefit in order to obtain a less rewarding but more immediate benefit.

DELAYED / DEFERRED GRATIFICATION.

This term refers to the act of resisting an impulse to take an immediately available reward in the hope of obtaining a more valued reward in the future.

The ability to delay gratification is a product of self-discipline; it is not something that people are naturally inclined to lean towards.

The story of the three little pigs is an overview of the above concept. The difference is seen in all areas of life; those that invest more in planned, focussed effort, reap more in results.

One cannot expect to make withdrawals in life when deposits have not been made. The pigs all had a choice regarding how they wanted to go about building their houses; the first two did it based on ease and convenience, whereas the third pig built it based on producing the best work.

We see the differences between immediate benefit and delayed benefits. It illuminates the perspective of making decisions that are based on new ideas.

Never let convenience dictate your preferences.

Our society is now intentionally geared towards various addictions, and instant/immediate gratification is one of them. Criminals operate this way because they lack any ability to delay the gratification process.

Think Social Media - so many now get their kicks out of dopamine from relatively little, to no real work done, all in the name of "likes."

After years of tweaking... of allowing myself to be wrong,
...of learning from mistakes, dealing with people and adapting to market conditions.

The most painful part, of all those years, were all the sacrifices that I had to make in acquiring the knowledge and the know-how, in order to execute and successfully build something awesome.

What got to me was dealing with how I felt like I was a failure for lagging behind. Although I wouldn't say I was a failure, it isn't a good feeling to start to realize that the things you want won't always happen according to your timeline.

In that time, you have to want what you want so badly that you put up with the pain, so much so that you become obsessed with accomplishing it.

Without that obsessive desire, you won't develop the fuel, energy and momentum you need to carry you through to the end. I've seen obsessive desire unlock tenacity and relentlessness and ultimately ...Success!

Many others that I knew seemed to fast track their way to corporate success. I was never against what others did; it just wasn't for me.

I knew that I would not be able to withstand a corporate environment, and above all else, I desired freedom and the money to make my own choices regarding life. No disrespect to those that have chosen that path, they too have a tough walk to success. The path for me was the more unknown and lonely path of creating and building my own things.

The main reason people don't get what they want in life is that they don't know what they want, and if they do, they often choose to try and shortcut the process.

I knew what I wanted was worth having, and I was willing to pay the price for it, no matter how long it took and no matter what I had to go through. Success is more a product of endurance than it is a product of skills or luck. I think the formula is 10% direction, 20% skill and 70% endurance (patience, perseverance and persistence.)

If you're willing to stake it out, then you'll get there, but most decide to give up along the way. You need to sacrifice short term pleasures and push on for what you really want because it is achievable.

Delay gratification and say hello to lasting success. Getting there is not as important as staying there.

The people who win big in life are the people who can forgo short term pleasures and play the long game by somehow developing an ability to create a mental distance in their need for gratification. These people build systems that facilitate freedom and go on and build more.

Those that do this are able to chase huge goals and endure tremendous pain in an arduous journey to attain the glory that comes with realizing massive goals. The long-term approach is able to absorb all flaws and errors in order to create what most see at the end as perfection.

An inability to delay gratification makes chasing big goals impossible; this is because the short-sighted game is too focused on quick results. Quick results often force a person to live in a loop of an absolute state of panic and rush.

Nature takes its time, yet everything is accomplished.

The last pig built with long term mindset and this saw him survive the wolf and profit off his brothers (I assume he charged them rent after this or at least opened a construction company) and made his mother proud.
He endured ridicule, exercised discipline and patience and was well rewarded.

The story implies choice,
it implies desire,
it implies sacrifice
and vision.

The story of the pigs holds a lot of lessons in it, as do all other old tales. Make some time and revisit them looking for wisdom you might have missed.

An additional lesson here, I think, is the fact that life eventually reveals all that is hidden. What is done in the dark will always be revealed in the light. You might feel like a loser and a failure now, but that is a good indication that you're either onto something big or downright ridiculous. Real massive progress demands the outcome of both these possibilities. In today's world, the late bloomer always at one stage appeared to resemble a failure.

Chapter 7

SUCCESS AND FAILURE

The only version of success you ought to be living is the one you've chosen for yourself.

"Success and failure are on the same road; success is just a little further down the road."
- Jack Hyles

VII

The term "success" has caused much anxiety. Much about the concept has changed, and subtly morphed over the years.

Just a few decades ago, some would have considered being happily married with a single source middle income as "success", today that is no longer the case.

Different stages of our collective human evolution require different sets of skills and different contribution. These different stages make our concept of "objective success" change over time.

Failure, on the other hand, is the opposite of what success is at that given time. Failure is something most try to avoid at all costs, and sadly it is something that many eventually succumb to.

Nobody wants to be perceived as a failure! Everybody wants to be successful in some way or the other. I have never heard of a person who intentionally wants to be a failure; failure itself isn't something you have to work towards, it is an automatic occurrence, if you do nothing about anything you wish to do. It requires no energy to fail.

The first thing I want to consider regarding success is a definition. Earl Nightingale had a go at this in his iconic video of 1968 called "the strangest secret", but I'd like to update it a little.

He said: "Success is the progressive realization of a worthy ideal."

I want to update that now to: "Success is the progressive realization of a subjectively chosen worthy ideal."

To break it down, for easy explanation:

Progressive realization: It is an on-going process that you can identify within your being. Progressive realization is not a destination that you one day reach.

Subjectively chosen worthy ideal: It something you choose personally. Nobody can define it for you. Your "subjectively chosen worthy ideal" is something specific and special to you.

What my updated definition means is that success is something intentional. It does not stop and can only be judged or identified by you in a personal sense. Only you can decide or know if you are successful or not.

The problem with the world is that the "collective unconscious" as Carl Jung puts it, continues to define what success should be. To a point where a rubric is created under which most people live, only to later wonder, why it is when they conform to the given ideas of success, they do not feel successful.

Albert Einstein had a quote that said: "If you judge a fish by its ability to climb a tree, it will live its whole life believing it is stupid."
Looking back at my life, I remember seeing so many peers I knew during my schooling who were made to feel like failures because they couldn't get the marks the so-called smart kids used to get. If you got A's, you were smart, and if you got a D or an E, you were just average. Tragically, many kids had their identities ingrained into them using this logic.

We were not taught how to think but only how to memorize mostly useless facts, to regurgitate them in a controlled test environment! ...and we call that education!

Have you also now come to the shocking realization that we were not taught anything remotely pertaining to life at school? Was this intentional, I wonder?

The word "education" itself comes from the Latin word "educo" which means to bring from within. There seems to be nothing worth mentioning to indicate that the current education system is successfully bringing anything out of people.

All I've seen is an exclusionary, outdated and classist system that is built on giving out badges for obedience and pushing away or pushing down those who refuse or can't conform to it.

I figured that surely there must've been a greater plan to life and not what we've been taught to live under. If we agree to what is in front of us, then what we are saying is that your fate in life is determined or decided mostly by the privileges or lack thereof from the moment you are born. Your family situation determines the conditions that you undergo in your education over the years.. My point is that creation itself surely had a higher plan or purpose with each of our lives that supersedes all that we've been taught to accept and believe.

I don't know where you find yourself reading this. As I'm writing this, I am on a plane, while my partner is passed out asleep, head on my shoulder.

I want you to know that if the world has made you believe less about yourself, then you are living a lie. What matters is what you define yourself to be! (as corny as that may sound.)

If you were an average or below standard student in high school or post-high school, that does not have to be your destiny.

You can lie to the whole world, but one thing you definitely cannot do is lie to yourself.
Lying, either way, is not good, but lying to yourself is as low as you can go.

How you began in this world does not have to be how you end up in this world. As a child, you are not responsible for the programming and circumstances you are born into; but as an adult, it is 100% your responsibility to undo that which does not align with who and what you wish to be. The only thing you need to do is DECIDE that it has to be different. Desire it with all of your might. See yourself wanting it and actually being moved into the action of making it happen.

The only version of success you ought to be living is the one you've chosen for yourself. Only your vision for yourself will grant you the feeling of happiness or fulfilment you seek.

Living someone else's idea of success will never grant you peace because you will always be chasing an idea of something that can never be reached; the process cannot be cheated. You owe nobody anything when it comes to your life and your happiness; not your parents, not your spouse, not your family and not your friends. You only owe it to yourself to make something out of yourself that you can be proud of. That will automatically benefit them.

So many people live day to day doing all that they can to appease their families, friends and loved ones. They do everything in their power to live up to the standards of those they have been taught to deem in high regard by virtue of birth, environment and circumstance. They make decisions, fearing the criticism of those they love and are loved by. They succumb to living under the expectations of others, seeking their approval and letting everyone else define what success in their lives should be (even if most of these people haven't done or achieved anything noteworthy in their lives.)

We definitely are a people that are quick to offer advice to others that we don't live under ourselves.

The moment you don't live blindly under the expectations of those who claim to love you, can you truly be you. Some of them might still consider you a failure, an outcast or delusional... but you will know the truth.

Here's a golden rule: Living out your own version of success according to the definition I have set out at the beginning of this chapter is going to come at a price of being in conflict with your immediate environment. Expect it and do not be surprised by it.

George Bernard Shaw said: "reasonable people adapt themselves to the world and unreasonable people adapt the world to themselves". You are going to have to be comfortable with being misunderstood, criticized and ridiculed for wanting more and better for yourself that is on your own terms. People won't like you for being bold enough to be who you've always wanted to be, but life will love you.

It is strange how people would prefer that you remain unhappy in hopes of maintaining the narrative they hold of you, rather than to see you go after the things you really want. Things that are geared and catered to make you happy and fulfil you. People that are consciously or unconsciously uncomfortable with you wanting the best for you and you boldly going for it are not your people! These people have hitched a free ride in your life, and that needs to come to an end!

Success is something that you're going to have to define for yourself and decide you want for yourself. It is not a destination but something that you must be moving towards on a daily basis. That means if you want to be an actor/actress, being successful is something that you do marginally that must move you in that direction on a daily basis and not the day you actually act on a big-time movie. This means success is a state we live under that moves us on a daily basis rather than a one-time event. This is why you only fail when you quit.

Most people want to be successful but expect it all to happen in a day, and success demands that you earn your stripes. What you must understand is that all of the choices in your life have led you to the point that you find yourself reading this. Where you are going from today will be determined by the choices you make from here on out. This means success or failure comes down to daily choices, what this also means is that you can decide to be successful from where you are right now; all it takes is a new set of decisions.

Decide to make a habit of choosing your path and then taking action.

You become what you constantly think about, what you talk about repeatedly and believe that spurs you into what you act out on a daily basis.

This means that signing up for that acting class and actively attending classes already makes you successful, buying and reading a book about acting makes you successful, starting to practice in front of the mirror makes you successful, attending auditions makes you successful.

Success is all the actions you take inline of the direction you wish to take for your life. These actions eventually compound so powerfully that people see you, years later, as an "overnight success." The next level of your life is not foreign to your current level; instead, it is an escalation of a process that is already in motion. This means the greatest expression of who you want to be, you already are or have access to in your current reality in a lesser form (even though it may not appear to be so.) Never despise the day of small beginnings, because little by little a little becomes a lot; this is why you must adopt the mindset of delayed gratification.

The problem with most people is that they don't want to be seen to be beginners, and they simultaneously don't want to apply enough consistency to breach the beginner phase. But every master was once a beginner.

The "money" is a result of mastering the state known as success. This is why much of the time, you will be successful while you are struggling and broke. The world will only catch up with you years later because success operates on the iceberg effect; it is massive underneath the surface before it breaches the surface and you are then deemed to have "made it."

On your journey to success, you will be met with many temporary failures; this is nothing strange but something that you should expect, this is just feedback that tells you to adapt your methods while staying on course with the vision. You only permanently fail when you give up. There is a process, it does take time, and there are no shortcuts, it will happen for you when you are ready and have put in the effort and refined your approach, not when you think you are ready. A blessing before your time that you cannot handle becomes a curse.

You alone must define what you deem to be success in your own life, and you will be successful the day you decide to start living it and not the day you reach it.

Never accept the world's conditions for success or failure because those are forever changing. The moment you adapt yourself to these conditions you will find yourself trying to live up to conditions that the masses are constantly changing based on how they are swayed by the outside stimuli that they get from the media, society etc.

The masses in history have always been wrong, so expect resistance and have the audacity to stand for what you believe in because your dreams are valid.

Chapter 8

FEAR

What stops you from reaching your full potential is the story you tell yourself

"What you are afraid to do is a clear indication of the next thing you need to do."
- Ralph Waldo Emerson

VIII

I watched a movie years ago called "After Earth" with Will Smith and his son as the main characters. It is a pretty average movie, but what stood out for me was this monster called the "Ursa" that was chasing them. The "Ursa" is a bio-engineered monster designed to kill humans; it hunts them by tracking the chemical secretions associated with a fear response. If you have no fear, you become invisible to the Ursa, but the greater your fear, the stronger your scent is to the Ursa.

I remember a quote from the movie where Will Smith says: "Fear is not real. It is a product of thoughts you create of the future. Do not misunderstand me, danger is very real, but fear is a choice." This is where I want to start this important chapter.

We were born with only two fears, first; the fear of heights and the fear of sudden loud noises. Every other fear from there we inherited somehow.

Both these innate fears relate to real potential danger and not the concept of illusionary fear this chapter will address.

We have all felt that feeling of fear that stops us from doing so many things we really want to do. Is it not tragically funny how fear never stops us from doing the things we don't want to do, but only those we want to do?

In high school and my early 20s, I was rather scared and awkward with many things, and that caused me to seek attention for all the wrong reasons at the time.

I am a completely different person from who I was in high school when it comes to fear, and I've come to understand fear from a different perspective. Fear is nothing more than an awareness of your own capabilities and the limits of your own strength based on past experience. Fear is basically a feeling that tells you that the current situation at hand is something you have not encountered before and thus have no guarantee of the outcome. Bear in mind that the feeling is more an indicator of what I said in the previous sentence than a hindrance, an indicator of a new direction you have never ventured into and not one you ought to avoid. This is something you must grasp!

What stops you from reaching your full potential is the story you tell yourself regarding the current situation right in front of you. I have seen that this is because of our past programming that I spoke of in the previous chapter. How you relate to yourself enormously determines how you relate to the world. If you tend to have a pessimistic view towards yourself, you will tend to have a pessimistic view towards life, in this case, fear will rule most of your decisions, and you won't amount to much. Similarly, he or she who possesses an optimistic view of themselves, tends to adopt an optimistic view of life. Optimism will allow one to bypass the feeling of fear and move on to occupy a greater, more successful space in reality.

I must reiterate, that fear is nothing but an indicator, but you alone decide whether or not you are influenced by it. It also has to be said that the people that you see making it in the world are not exempt or immune from the feeling of fear. They too experience it anytime they wish to do new things. Their primary defence against fear is that they are optimistic about the future and thus never allow it to control their narrative. You are either telling yourself a good story about yourself daily, or you're telling yourself a bad story about yourself. I doubt heaven or hell is a place one goes to after one dies, I believe heaven or hell is a reality one is forced to also experience on Earth based on the mindsets they subscribe to.

Because the majority accepts the programs laid out by society, they naturally succumb to their fears and thus project those fears onto everyone else. Society has its own embedded policing systems that automatically engage when anyone tries to believe in anything different from the group. Think of the classic "crabs in the bucket" theory.

Napoleon Hill mentioned six fears humankind is ruled under in his book "Outwitting the Devil."

The six fears humankind is plagued by in order from most dominant to least dominant:

1. The fear of poverty
2. The fear of criticism
3. The fear of ill health
4. The fear of loss of love
5. The fear of old age
6. The fear of death

* The fear of poverty forces people to make decisions geared towards security instead of prosperity. This fear never allows people to take

risks at all because they believe if they do, they will lose. This fear also opens up people to being scammed by the "get rich quick" schemes that prey on desperation.

* The fear of criticism forces people to tend to conform, rather than to pave their own way because they fear what will be said of them. This fear is at the core of why people do so much to try and impress others, even at the expense of their own happiness.

* The fear of ill health forces people to do all they can to avoid adverse health conditions. They do this not knowing that the mere act of doing all you can to try to avoid ill health is actually causing one to focus on the fear. This misdirected focus is precisely what attracts negative health conditions. In this sense, I am not saying that one should not focus exclusively on health; what I am saying is that one should not obsess over it. Your body is built to self-regulate itself, and it wants to keep you alive too.

* The fear of loss of love is the fear that turns people into jealous, and obsessive people who believe that they cannot get or do better in the category of love. This fear forces people to stay in relationships that hurt them all in the name of familiarity, even if they are unhappy. This fear is at the core of abuse and lack of trust in relationships.

* The fear of old age forces people to focus so much on their outward appearance to a point where they are willing to part with copious amounts of money to avoid looking older even though this is a natural order of things. This fear also forces people to make irrational decisions as they get older and is the source of a mid-life crisis. This fear makes people feel like they have missed out on life and that they cannot do anything with their lives because they no longer young anymore.

* The fear of death forces people to focus so much on the afterlife that they neglect the life they are living right now. This fear also

gives rise to superstition and sometimes an over-commitment to religion not from the perspective of growth and understanding but from the perspective of fearing a deity; this opens up people to being scammed, used and give in to dangerous cult-like belief systems.

Each one of these fears cripples humankind during their time here, and this is something that you must be aware of. Behind most of these fears, you will find a corresponding industry that exists to anticipate this fear and profit from it.

For the fear of poverty: Life insurance and Ponzi schemes.

For the fear of criticism: Corporate systems that expect conformity.

For the fear ill health: Medical insurance, big pharma etc.

For the fear of loss of love: Tv Shows, love gurus and the rise of things such as love potions.

For the fear of old age: Plastic surgery

For the fear of death: Widespread religion and cults.

Remedies:

* Regarding the fear of poverty – decide that you will make it a point accumulate wealth responsibly without harming others and that you will get along with the wealth you are going to accumulate and maintain it. Think of it as a decision to focus less on what could go wrong and to focus more on what could go right as a result of the decision you took to be intentional about your finances. Decide from this that you will be in control of your finances and commit yourself to the study of money and its many mechanisms. People go

broke not because of what they know but because of what they don't know or don't apply.

* Regarding the fear of criticism – decide to stop worrying about what others think of you and to be sure that you think correctly regarding yourself. Most people are so busy living their lives with their own stresses to waste time thinking about you and how you are living your life. Even if they do; they will get sucked back into their own lives very quickly; so don't base your life decisions because of moments of conflict. Don't take yourself too seriously.

* Regarding the fear of ill-health – decide to focus more on positive health than on negative health. Give the body the proper food, water, sunlight and exercise it requires, and it should regulate itself. Also, be wary of your body and be able to pick up when something happens to it and then apply the required correcting measure. The body will always whisper before it screams. Do your best to clear your mind of diseases and the symptoms you hear on the news; I am not saying that these things are not real but what I am saying is once again, for you not to put your focus on these things lest you increase the power of this fear. Practise a healthy lifestyle, and this will require you once again, to do some research for yourself.

* Regarding the fear of the loss of someone's love – decide to enjoy, cherish and value the people in your life that love you and make sure that you return the love they give you because these people won't always be around. When you're alone, do not think that nobody wants to be with you but know that there are people out there who are for you but you must make sure that you take good care of yourself, love yourself first before you pursue these people.

* Sure some people might be spoilt for choice and attractiveness is something that you may or may not fall into in an objective sense and that is ok. To attract people, you must become an attractive

person to yourself and conduct your life in such a way that clearly demonstrates to others that you value yourself.

* Regarding the fear of old age – decide to accept that old age is inevitable, a part of life and as a blessing. Not everyone gets to grow old, and that is something you must be aware of and be grateful for. Be willing to freely give the next generation the wisdom you have acquired over the years. This will do more for them than you think.

* Regarding the fear of death – The fear of death is not something I can prescribe to you because we deal with it in our own way based on our beliefs regarding it. What I will say however is to learn to cherish people while they are here and to let them know what they mean to you before it is too late. Death is something we cannot escape and a destination we all will meet one day and so it is imperative to live your life in such a way that you value and use your time in such a way that you are ready to go at any moment.

I once read a quote that said: "He that is ready to die is he that begins to live."

Marcus Aurelius said: "You act like mortals in all that you fear, and like immortals in all that you desire."

We certainly aren't here forever, and so we must make it a point to use the time we have on Earth.

Fear is not a real thing; it is just the story you have been taught to tell yourself that does nothing but stop you from getting the results you seek if you give in to them. The truth is that your fears are mostly imaginary; the past hurts you because of memory and the future hurts you in your imagination. None of these are real in the present moment. Fear is an imaginary concept that you have been taught to operate from as a result of years and years of programming. You must constantly be aware of this!

Fear is not something you did to yourself but something that was programmed into you by society, or by the environment you grew up in. It happened to you without your knowledge or initial consent, but now it is your responsibility from this day forward to make the active choice not to be a person that is ruled by fear. Fear is standing in the way of you starting to go after everything you want. Be aware, though, that this process of shedding your fears doesn't happen overnight, nor is it a once-off set of choices; it is a constant process, but it starts with being aware of your own inner enemy.

You must be willing to unlearn what you have been programmed to believe from birth. That software no longer serves you if you want to live in a world where all things are possible.

I left the chapter on fear for last in Part one because it is critical that you understand the enemy that you've been up against, whether you were aware of it or not, has always been against you and the impotent version of you that you've allowed yourself to operate from.

Your enemy is not society but the person standing in front of you in the mirror. Only he or she who becomes aware of their chains can aspire to freedom.

Part one was to make you aware of the chain's society has placed onto you with or without your knowledge. These chains have been the sole reason for the mindset you've adopted that has halted and sometimes sabotaged your progress. These are the things that you need to unlearn.

I will repeat that you must be willing to unlearn what you have been programmed to believe from birth. That software no longer serves you if you want to live in a world where all things are possible.

PART TWO

LEARNING

Chapter 9

DESIRE

Most never admit the things they want

"The implanting of a desire indicates that its gratification
is in the constitution of the creature that feels it."
- Ralph Waldo Emerson

IX

Do you believe the things you want are possible to attain? Or are you hoping for some things but aren't sure if they'd manifest, so it remains just a nice to have? Are you leaving your dream aside because it isn't worth the disappointment to actually really want it and not get it?

Most never admit the things they want, and if by some stroke, they do, they don't have the killer instinct to actually claim the things they want out of life. Most people seem to aim low with the things they want because that's what they believe is possible to them. Once again, this is a programming issue that has been involuntarily instilled in us.

Child experts claim that a toddler hears the word "no" about 400 times a day and as the years go by you can imagine how many more times you would've heard the word "no" over the word "yes." I by no means am saying that parents (even mine) should have said "yes" to me every time. But if "no" was what formed most of your results; it would eventually kill anyone's desire to ask for anything simply because of an expectation that is based upon past experience. As a result, we have a natural inclination to develop a negative, pessimistic view of reality. Our past results set the basis today, for where we wish to aim tomorrow. As I said before, people would rather aim low or settle for what they can get than to risk disappointment.

THINKING BIG

This is easier said than done, but the things you want are evidence of the available power within you to achieve the result. "Ask, and you shall receive" is the law and Napoleon Hill also said: "whatever the mind can conceive and believe, it can achieve."

The limitations you now hold, are all self-imposed and made to appear real by the influences you have allowed to impinge on your idea of what is possible. You are capable of much more than what you currently believe, and the moment you open yourself up to this reality, the more space you will be forced to occupy in the realm of possibilities. The mind can only be what it knows and believes it can be, and the body is then tasked to accomplish that which the mind believes.

The only things that are not possible are the things you believe are not possible, and by Universal Law, it is then done unto you as you believe (every action has an equal, similar and opposite reaction). The only antidote to this state of smallness is to start thinking big. If this is too much to ask, then start by at least raising the bar of what you want in life. You will have to be radical in your approach, and you'll know you've done this correctly when you can create new problems for yourself and have people around you doubt your ability to do it.

You want people around you to be concerned about what you want to achieve because it is only then when you know you have gone beyond crowd programming. If you continue to live within the confounds of what the crowd deems possible, you will remain exactly where they are forever, which is NOT where you want to be by virtue of you buying this book!

It is ok to want it...

The reason most people never get what they want is because they don't know what they want! They never decide on it, and as an inevitable result, they never go after it, and that means they will never have it! It really is that simple.

When digging deep into the issue, you find that most don't believe they are worthy of amazing things, riches or a remarkable life with deep, meaningful relationships. Nobody has ever told them its ok to want the things they want. What this does, is force a person to live life either looking down or horizontally all around them while instilling an automatic fear of looking up; for that would mean immediate repudiation and criticism from the crowd which stems from one of the six fears previously mentioned.

I repeat ...it is ok to want the things that you want.

It is ok to want the things that you feel are beating off of the edge of your heart. These desires are real simply because you can imagine them (imagination creates reality.) What is even more important for you to know is that you are worthy of these desires. You don't have to settle for a second-rate life simply because that is what the majority of those around you experience. Their limits are theirs and not yours. Your task is to go higher than this and to dare to chart your own course in the life you wish to live.

BE OBSESSED.

One last thing I want to add to this before we wrap up the chapter is for you to understand "obsession". For too long the word has had a negative connotation attached to it that we associated with psycho lovers and totally deranged people. What I want you to understand is that a true desire is deeply etched into your heart and is the real authenticity of who you are! It is going to be the most difficult yet the most rewarding journey you can undertake, and it is going to take everything.

You must allow yourself to want what you want; to love what you want; to go after but to also become wholeheartedly obsessed with it. Only an insane obsession will get you through the days when rationality will make the average person quit and give up. Your desire must be strong enough to make you operate beyond reason, beyond logic and beyond what most deem rational. The moment you can do this, you will be able to automatically withstand everything you encounter because you will understand that everything is temporary, that everything you go through is preparing you for what you asked for. Some of this will only make sense to you when you look back. Balance only comes later.

People who pursue their destinies have lives that make sense when they look back and reflect; they understand WHY certain things had to happen the way they did. They also understand that every adversity added to some benefit they experienced only later.

GO FOR IT!

From this day forward, you are going to make up your mind on EXACTLY what you want, and you are going to go after it regardless of who gets upset with you for adopting that approach to life. Deepak Chopra said it beautifully when he said: "Inherent in every intention or desire are the mechanics of its fulfilment."

Chapter 10

THE POWER OF THINKING

Our thoughts shape our world

"You must learn a new way to think before
you can master a new way to be."
- Marianne Williamson

X

We have all heard quotes and wonderful sayings regarding our thinking and how we ought to control our thoughts. I have listened to people waffle on and then go on to loosely mention things such as "meditation". I often wonder if these people really know what all this loose advice really means. I'm not saying they are wrong, but I question if they know what the things they say mean.

The truth that I have discovered about most quotes that are deemed to be cliché is that THEY ARE ALL TRUE! There is a reason why they have rampaged through society over the years and said in countless different ways by countless different people. The only problem with cliché quotes and sayings is that they have been said so many times that often the value of the wisdom is lost because it all becomes a sort of mental wallpaper.

Our thoughts shape our world or let me rather say that the thoughts we allow to harden in our minds become the very experiences we must encounter in the place we call reality. You will always gravitate towards and become the crystallisation of your most dominant thoughts.

For as long as we are awake, our consciousness is bombarded with media and other material which forces us to think. Something someone says to you, the radio, the TV, the text from your phone, a post you see on social media, a song that you hear, and the list goes on. You can't count how many advertisements you are exposed to daily.

ATTENTION

As soon as some external stimuli catch your attention, you automatically direct your awareness towards it and are forced to form a thought regarding it. You then build onto it, another corresponding thought reacting or responding to the stimuli based on your own built-in response systems.

If you see an ad for a car, when you don't need or want a car, you will automatically dismiss that ad and carry on with your life, whereas if you see an ad for cheap flights to a destination you have been looking to go to, you will more than likely take further action towards that ad. It's really about what you are ready to receive and your core programming that will determine whether or not you accept or reject the stimuli that is now in front of you.

Big brands pay Marketing and PR companies billions annually to fight for your attention, and the moment you understand the power and the value of your attention, you will stop giving it away so cheaply.

AIMLESS DRIFTING

The question that now arises as we stress the importance of your thoughts is, who controls your thinking? It's a terrifying question to ask because the answer might not be something that one might want to admit to themselves, but that doesn't mean that it can't be asked.

The vast majority of citizens refuse to do their own thinking and as a result, allow society to do their thinking for them. They play a game of "follow the follower" and do the same things at the same time without a known reason for why they are doing it. The answer you'll get most of the time for why they do what they do is "everybody else is doing it."

You notice how terribly attached these people are to the lives they automatically live by how ready they are to attack you as soon as you think and then act differently to them. All of a sudden, you become the focal point because your mere rebellion forces them to adapt to and challenges the narrative they hold about their own lives.

Almost like the attack you get from people when you tell them you don't drink or aren't planning to drink at that time, it's almost as if you not drinking, causes an upset to their lives.

The state of living life according to society and merely following the rules is called "aimless drifting". Hopelessly moving through life and letting life make choices for you without a single intention, especially in the major issues of life.

Many loosely give away control when making decisions about what to do with their lives. This results in them choosing the safest and most secure careers that guarantee income; not being aware that those careers are usually based on what society deems important and necessary at any given point in time.

Many others allow society to decide who they should date, when they should marry, under what circumstances they should marry and how to go about their married lives. The people you choose to allow into your inner circle are the most important people in your life; that selection process has to be strict and not a free for all!

Here's a rule that I want you to instil in your life: EVERYTHING THAT IS WORTH HAVING IN THIS LIFE REQUIRES INTENTIONAL EFFORT TO ACQUIRE AND THEN ONGOING EFFORT TO MAINTAIN!

You don't just wake up in shape; you work your way into shape with exercise and a planned diet. You don't wake up with a fat bank account one day, you organise yourself and create a product or service people need that you can deliver to them in an organised, neat way that they are prepared to pay you for. You don't wake up with awesome relationships; you make the necessary effort to communicate and make time for the people who matter to you.

So many want all these amazing things to happen to them, yet they assume that these things happen automatically, and as soon as things fall apart, they still wonder why. Here is another golden rule:

Misery is easy and common because it is the default, but happiness requires effort, and that is why it is rare.

CONFORMITY

I remember once coming across a story about a little girl who watched her mom make a full chicken in the oven. Before she put the chicken in the oven, she removed the drumsticks, wings and only put the body in the oven. This must have seemed strange to the little girl (probably she had seen it many times before), and so she then asked her mother why she was doing this?

Her mom, perplexed, answered that she had no idea; she had seen her own mother cook the chicken like that. The puzzled mother asked her daughter to go ask her grandmother why she cooked a whole chicken like that.

The little girl's grandmother upon being asked, was also perplexed and said that she too had seen her own mother cooking like that, and that was why she cooked it in that manner.

The grandmother then tasked the little girl to go to her great grandmother (who was luckily still alive) and ask her the same question. When the little girl asked her great grandmother the question, she simply said that she has no idea why the little girl's mother did this, but she had to do it like that because in her day ovens were so small that a full chicken could never fit! All ovens nowadays are large enough to fit at least three entire chickens in, wings and drumsticks and all.

Crazy story I know...

You are an individual, and that is something that you need to come to terms with right now. You are not a "copy" of others. No, you are more than that! Conforming to what everyone else around you is doing is suicide to that part of you that believes that all things are possible. You might not know or believe that part in you exists, but it never goes away, it only lies dormant, waiting for the day you decide to stop going through life betraying yourself by wearing a mask, trying to be everything you deep down inside, KNOW you are not.

Conforming to the crowd will make you a statistic because your choices automatically put you in the same pool everyone else makes their decisions from, and everyone gets wet from the same water.

You do not want to be like people who refuse to think for themselves and consume everything mainstream. Everything they can be, want, or aspire to be is dictated to them by dogma - the media, by family, by those who came before them and by the people they spend most of their time with, as in the story of the little girl. They are all in the same sinking boat and yet trying to act like they aren't.

BEING INTENTIONAL AND SELECTING YOUR THOUGHTS

You must decide from this day forward that you are going to be the person that decides where your life must head. You are no longer going to live life as a wave that is tossed around by the wind. You are going to get in control of your thinking and become intentional about your life because that is the place you begin.

We become what we think about, and this means that you are going to make an active effort to decide what you will think.

Everything in your daily life contains material with which you will use to do your thinking; you become powerful only when you begin to become aware and then selective with what you allow to influence your thinking.

The first step is withdrawal; this means you must start off by removing the sources that have been feeding you the limiting information that you have used to think from.

You are going to switch off the radio; you are going to stop watching the news, stop reading newspapers and mainstream articles. You are going to cancel all TV and streaming subscriptions that you have to the degree that works for you because I know this is not an easy thing. You can add these back once you feel you are making progress.

The news is geared to stir negative shock emotion in you to gain your attention so that you buy into the publication and also reinforce the programming. I used to make it a point to listen to the news because I thought I was gaining some knowledge about the world and that it would make me smarter. Then I realised that most of the news is bad news, and it affected my mood. One can't load up on murders, deaths and robberies in the morning and then expect to have a happy cheery day afterwards. You reap what you sow.

This first step is crucial because it will begin the process of making you feel better about yourself by controlling what you take into your subconscious. What you allow to come inwardly, you must express outwardly. You will notice how being in a bad mood negatively affects everything that you do afterwards; a bad mood makes good food taste bad!

Note: You don't have to be extreme and make the first step arduous for yourself, but you must work with yourself at a comfortable pace you can handle, but still push yourself.

My whole aim is to make you aware of the fact that you need to drastically cut down and eventually eliminate everything that has been controlling your thinking without your awareness. Remember this is your life and all the wisdom in this book is a ladder, but it is you who must get yourself up the ladder. Once you get comfortable with the first step, proceed to the next rung, but work with yourself because the process does not happen overnight.

The second step is to replace the space you have created in the above step with things that uplift you and make you feel better about your life and actually improve you. It will all feel weird to you at first, because you've grown accustomed to being influenced by the things that have been influencing you and this is ok, it is normal. This second step doesn't have to be drastic, but where you were listening to the news, you must replace this with something soothing such as music, silence or a podcast.

You could replace watching the news with watching a thought-provoking movie but not series, as series takes too much time and is designed to keep you wanting more. You can get back to watching series' once you have a tight grip on yourself. The aim here is for you to decide when you want to be entertained and not for entertainment itself to determine when you should be entertained — everything on your own terms.

The thinking that guides your responses is more important than any new intelligence gained by itself.

Chapter 11

SELF IMAGE PSYCHOLOGY

Nothing changes unless you change!

"Change your conception of yourself, and you will automatically change the world in which you live. Do not try to change people; they are only messengers telling you who you are. Revalue yourself, and they will confirm the change."
- Neville Goddard

XI

What do you think of yourself? Do you think of yourself as a powerful person who goes after what they want and gets it? Do you think of yourself as a person who doesn't want to bump against the world too much for fear of standing out?

Everyone is talking about success in this day and age, there is a big frenzy about it all, and this has led many people down the path of trying strategy after strategy with no luck or results. Many of these "programs" and "courses" miss one simple yet critical fact:

Nothing changes unless YOU change!

It was James Allen who said that many people are anxious to improve their circumstances but are unwilling to improve themselves. Eventually, I found out that you do not attract what you want, but you attract what you are. For different results, you don't fight to change circumstances, you fight to change yourself. If you don't change the roots, you will keep encountering the very same fruit they produce.

All circumstances that one encounters are there to reveal you to yourself. They are an outpouring or a crystallisation of a collection of your thoughts over a specific period of time. This is why the chapter on thinking had to precede this chapter.

Being able to be selective about your thoughts is the first step to real power; the second step to real power is to possess the ability to think yourself into a new state of being.

I learnt a long time ago that the real prize is not the prize you achieve, the real prize is the person you have to become in order to get the prize, that is the true value. In this case, you do not chase success; instead, you chase to become a person of value; this will automatically attract people, opportunities and inevitable success towards you and keep them. Getting there is not as important as staying there.

The key point here is this: It's about WHO you become and not what you do. What you can do is an automatic extension of who you are at any point in time.

It took me over eight years of trial and error to get my ideas right and turn them into a success. It took me two failed books to write this book which I know will get published. I can now build and create companies in a fraction of the time it took me to get here; what changed? The answer is simple: I changed. Hell, I can have everything taken from me, and I'll be able to get it back in less than a year. I now fully understand that success is a mindset you acquire, and then that mindset makes everything it is exposed to, successful.

What I'm trying to say to you is that in this world, you will lose many things; many things will be taken away from you to make way for other things, but nobody can take away who you are, and nobody can discredit or belittle who you think you are unless you allow it.

This means that your investment should mostly be in yourself and more importantly, into striving to become someone as opposed to trying to achieve something. You must become the person who is worthy of the goal you are seeking and only then will nature hand over the win to you. As I said before, you do not attract what you want in this life; you attract what you are.

First, you decide who you want to be; then act in line with the requirements that the mindset of such a person demands and then get all the accruals that person has a right to by virtue of who they are.

BE. DO. GET.

Most people assume this to be: Get. Do. Be!

As a result, they wait for the results or certain conditions to be met before they decide to act and hence never get to it simply because they are operating against basic principles.

I made the mistake of thinking I could stay the same person I was while being surrounded by the same people I was surrounded by when I went after the things I went after. Committing to change from the get-go will save you so much time accepting the changes that you must inevitably face in order to become the new person you have to be who is worthy of massive goals.

Chase a whole new theme for your life and not just goals. A theme is the feeling and idea of your life as a whole and is very specific; goals are just parts that form the whole theme.

Think yourself into a new reality and into a whole new person.

The world adapts to the belief you hold of yourself. The moment you think yourself into a higher state of being by raising your standards at the expense of your current lived experience, you will see over time, reality begins to meet you at your new chosen level.

I got to a point where I accepted that how I viewed myself was drastically different from what was around me and after facing a few failures, I had fundamentally changed. I had to let go of where I was because I didn't want it and staying there was more painful than attempting to go forward. There was nothing behind me, nothing much to miss, and that's why I left it alone. I accepted that I was not made to operate in low places, and as soon as I began to believe it, I started to operate in a higher realm. This obviously caused a rift in the majority of the people in my life, but at some point, you have to stop lying to yourself. You can lie to the world, but you cannot lie to yourself.

I look back at life now, and I can without a shadow of a doubt say that everything changed the moment I adopted a new higher thinking pattern regarding who I was. And this will be true for you too as soon as you adopt a higher idea of yourself.

Where you are right now, I want you to start exclaiming that you deserve way more than what you have currently been accepting and I want you to raise your standards in everything that you are, do and expect.

To be more, you must think more of yourself which will make you do more, and the result will be you having more.

Chapter 12

HABITS & SUBCONSCIOUS PROGRAMMING

Every Master was once a Beginner.

"The habits you created to survive will no longer serve you when it's time to thrive. Get out of survival mode, new habits, new life.'
- Ebonee Davis.

XII

I looked up the word "habit" in the dictionary, and the two definitions that stood out for me were:

"A settled or regular tendency or practice, especially one that is hard to give up."

"Something that you do often and regularly, sometimes without knowing that you are doing it."

The two crucial parts in the above definitions are the "hard to give up" part as well as the "sometimes without knowing that you are doing it" part.

Habits are divided mainly into two categories, good habits and bad habits. We can maybe also add poor people's habits as well as rich people habits just to really get into this topic.

In my journey, what got me to where I am today wasn't a few massive actions that I performed once in a while, no. It was a collection of what I did daily and consistently - a sequential string of events. I remember telling myself every week that on the Friday (end of the week), I must be further than what I was on the Monday (beginning of the week).

I also made it a point to read up at least 3-5 articles daily, which eventually led to me listening to podcasts as well as audiobooks almost on a daily basis. That level of incremental effort compounds over the years, and that is the most important lesson I've learnt when it comes to success or failure - The domino strategy that starts with one domino falling and starts a continuous chain of events.

Your whole life is predicated on what you do daily. People who exercise regularly will know this too. Someone will start working out today, and in 2-3 years the person is in shape, and people hate you because that process isn't microwavable. There was nothing magical or singular that happened; it was just a collection of habits compounded over time, and this is true of many areas of life, the compound effect is indeed powerful! Show me your daily habits, and I can show you to a large extent what your future will look like.

In chapter four, I spoke of being able to program yourself. In chapter ten, I told you that your reality is a crystallization of your thoughts, and in the preceding chapter on self-image, I told you about raising your standards. In this chapter, I want to extrapolate that process.

SUBCONSCIOUS PROGRAMMING

Your mind or psyche is made up of the conscious and subconscious mind. The conscious mind is your active approach to thinking and neural activity; this part of your thinking you control and is what helps you filter the barrage of stimuli that hits you on a daily basis. This part of our thinking we are aware of but only makes up at most 5% of our thinking daily as this takes a large amount of energy and concentration.

The subconscious mind is your automated and passive approach to thinking and neural activity. This automated thinking process takes care of our basic life functions (breathing, heartbeat), our behaviours, as well as our learned habits.

This is also where we house our personality, emotions, belief systems and approach to life. According to psychology, 95% of our thinking and behaviour is a result of habitual thinking which means that we carry 95% of yesterday's thinking/behaviour into today. Think of your subconscious mind as the version of you that is on autopilot and your conscious mind as being that part of you that is in control of the plane.

Autopilot systems are pre-programmed into a planes software, but when you take control of the plane, the plane responds to you.

We've often heard the phrase that said that human beings are creatures of habit. From our definition of habits, we see that there are things we do that are difficult to stop as well as things we do that, we are sometimes unaware that we are doing. Habits are then our automated approach to life, and if we are going to decide on an awesome course of life, it is then our personal habits that we need to be aware of at a subconscious level and make some adjustments where necessary.

REPETITION

They say it takes 21 days to create a habit and 90 days to create a new lifestyle. I don't know how scientifically correct the statement is but what I do know is that the subconscious mind can only be re-programmed by use of repetition. Aristotle said, "We are what we repeatedly do; and therefore, excellence is not an act but a habit."

The primary key to altering your life for the better comes from being able to take active control in your own thinking. You must direct that thinking into a new state of being. It is the selection and the performance of incremental and consistent actions that thus become a part of who you are over time. Many people start things only to give up on them before they become a thing simply because they hate being seen as beginners but simultaneously don't practice the new act long enough for it to become a habit. Every master was once a beginner.

There is no easy way to say this to you, and if you aren't committed to this process, then you might as well close this book right now and give it to someone else. This is a crucial piece of wisdom that you need to accept right now regarding life; IT ALL COMES DOWN TO YOUR HABITS!

A lot of people aren't even aware of their habits and how they play an active role in sabotaging them on a daily basis, and so I will repeat what I said above since we are talking about repetition repetition repetition; IT ALL COMES DOWN TO YOUR HABITS!

AFFIRMATIONS

The word "affirmation" comes from the Latin word: "affirmare" which means to affirm, assert, confirm, ratify, restore and emphasize.

I've heard the word "affirmations" being so casually thrown around by people.

The process of transformation must begin on the inside before it manifests itself on the outside. By now, I would assume you have really started to be honest with yourself and at least decided on what you want. Secondly, you've started to zero in on the person you wish to be who is worthy of those desires because that is a mandatory transformation. This is going to require you to subconsciously believe you are that person which will then translate into actions and habits that support your new believed conclusion.

It is said that the power of life and death is in the tongue and that the mouth speaks with the abundance of the heart (subconscious mind). This means that you now must start imagining and speaking the conclusion into your own being.

The subconscious mind cannot distinguish between what is real and what is imagined, which is why things such as masturbation are what they are. Reality is all happening inside of you and is projected outside of you. Whatever you believe regarding your life internally and who you are, you must then experience in the external world or reality; I won't go into why this is so because it will make this book lengthy, but for now, I want you to know this to be true and take it as is.

You are going to start off by having three sets of affirmations a day, one for the morning, one for the afternoon and one for the evening.

These affirmations are the new story you are going to start telling yourself based on your desires as well as the person you wish to become that you are now going to exclaim as being true. It is imperative that these affirmations be in a language and structure you understand, it doesn't help that you use big words and old language that you don't speak on a daily basis. The aim of this is for you to spark emotion in your words because the subconscious mind is impressed by emotion. So only use words you understand, that mean something to you; in other words, use your own words and your own way of speaking.

An example of this in the morning would be:

"Today Is going to be an awesome day. I am grateful for this day because I know that this day holds all the opportunities I want that will get me closer to where I am going.

Everything that happens to me is perfect and for my highest good. I am an amazing person who is healthy, wealthy and happy. Something incredible is on its way to me, and I, therefore, act accordingly today in order to prepare for it."

In the afternoon, it could be:

"Today is going exactly as my highest self needs it to go even though I might not understand it now. I am grateful for everything, and everything continues to happen for me in a way that benefits me."

In the evening, it could be:

"Thank you for this complete day. I did the best that I could do today, and I, therefore, go to sleep feeling accomplished. I will wake up tomorrow to new opportunities and will make the best decisions. I am happy, I am hungry for life, and I am a magnet for the abundance that is finding its way to me daily. People want to be around me, and I am a successful person. Thank you for everything."

These are examples, and there is no specific order or length they can be, but the main take away for you is that you write them down somewhere and write them down as if they are already accomplished and not something that must still happen. The longer you tell yourself something, the better; eventually, you'll start to believe it.

What works for me is that I write them in a note app on my phone, so I can look at them from time to time as I go along the way of my life; I also tend to update these over time because one must always update their belief system. You will see over time how the things you write about start to come into your life; the key is to stay ready to act, open and ready to receive and this is done through preparing with small actions in the direction of your desires. He that asks for success and prepares for failure must then experience failure.

Please note that it is important that the things you desire are closely etched to your heart, you must want what you want and who you want to be badly enough that you become obsessed with it and then write these affirmations around that.

It may also help to write down your desires and to also look at them from time to time, but I don't think anyone needs reminders of what they really want but writing things down and creating vision boards have proven to be effective for people and so I won't discount them; the aim of the game is for you to start creating a new reality for yourself from the inside out in the easiest way that works for you.

> "People do not decide their futures, they decide their habits and their habits decide their futures."
> - F.M. Alexander

Chapter 13

SELF-DISCIPLINE, ACTION AND MOMENTUM

All Excuses are Lies wrapped up in Reasons

"Self-discipline begins with the mastery of your thoughts. If you don't control what you think, you can't control what you do. Simply, self-discipline enables you to think first and act afterwards."
- Napoleon Hill

XIII

Regardless of what you want, how badly you want it and how happy it will make you; there is nothing worthwhile that can be achieved without self-discipline which is the ability to give yourself commands and actually follow them. It is only the people who are able to move themselves, that are able to move the world. Without self-discipline, you are the one that will be constantly being moved around by those who are able to move themselves.

How many people do we know that enrol in a gym in January, only to quit a few days or a few weeks later? I remember someone once saying that the only thing you need to do regarding gym, is to get yourself to the door, yet this task seems momentous to most people.

That life you want, that body you want, that relationship you want and that bank account you want, will only come through self-discipline. Even if you do manage to get the above desires by some other miraculous way, it still will require self-discipline in order to keep and maintain them. I have seen and know millionaires who made their money themselves or through the help of their parents, only to lose everything because of a lack of self-discipline. Sex, drugs, alcohol, gambling and other vices all were magnified when the money came, and they lacked self-discipline. This made me realize that no amount of money or success can help you when you are your worst enemy because you will take four steps forward, but your lack of discipline will take you eight steps back. Ensuring you have yourself under control through self-discipline should be one of your highest priorities. You have got to get yourself under control!

ACQUISITION OF SELF-DISCIPLINE

Self-discipline is simply the act of choosing between what you want now and what you want most later on.

If there is nothing that you want most in life, if you have no big goals, you will be forced to act based on what you want now. The vision for your life, which is greater than where you are now will impose discipline on you.

Once you have a powerful vision for your life, it then dictates your decisions from there on out.

There is no other way that I've seen that a human being can delay gratification without a solid reason or prize greater than that which is before him in the now.

Most choose to settle into a second-rate life and never reach their full potential. They don't go after what they want because they lack the discipline that helps them make all the decisions that will get them there.

They do this because they either don't know what they want or don't want what they want badly enough. They then live a life of making excuses blaming everything and everyone else for their unhappy lives. All excuses are lies wrapped up in reasons, and in this life, you are either going to spend time building the life you REALLY want that is in harmony and authentic to you, or you're going to be forced to spend a lot of time learning to deal with a life you don't want; there is no in-between.

The vision for your life is the most important thing you will own because that is tied to what you truly want for your life and it is the very thing that will grant you the discipline you need in order to get you where you want to get. This is why the most dangerous people to associate yourself with are those without direction because they already are where they want to be and when you don't know where you are going, any road will take you there.

You must know what you want, and you must want it BADLY enough, and this is why I always encourage people to raise their standards and to think big. It is only when you think big that you will birth a scary but exciting vision that will force you to rise to the challenge and transform yourself into a person who is worthy of the amazing goal you currently desire.

ACTION

Your thinking over time dictates your beliefs and emotions regarding stimuli, and it is that emotional response that spurs you into action. People think that it takes large actions to get them where they want to get, but as we all know, a journey of a thousand miles begins with one single step.

Regardless of how much you think you know, how much wisdom you have and how much you want what you want; without action you cannot claim it.

Right where you are now, you are going to have to start moving towards the very thing that scares you most.

It doesn't matter who thinks what about you; right now, where you are, you're going to make that decision to go after what you want. You will enrol into that class, you will sign up for that membership, you will slowly walk yourself out of that situation that makes you unhappy, you will make that call and send that email. It's all about the steps we take and not the leaps we hope to take.

Take the steps, bit by bit regardless of how long it takes and no's you will encounter along the way. You don't eat an elephant all at one go; you eat it one bite at a time.

I came to a stark realization when I was trying to make Lohocla a success, that the worst thing people could do when I called or emailed them was to say "No."

Even if they did, it would mean that someone new out there knew my name and at least knew about Lohocla.

Fear is a lie but also an indicator of the direction you want to head most. The moment you can feel scared but act anyway is when you stop living life on your knees.
You will start walking around life knowing you have the right to be here and that's the time that life starts to hand over to you EXACTLY what you want out of it! This happens because you have committed yourself to not backing down. You will not be stopped!

MOMENTUM

Isaac Newton's first law of motion or the law of inertia says that an object at rest tends to stay at rest and an object in motion tends to stay in motion with the same speed and in the same direction unless acted upon by an external force. This means that objects tend to keep on doing what they are doing.

If you are in motion and have formed the habit of acting and being in motion, you will tend to stay in motion, and the opposite holds true, and this is what momentum is.

You will either have positive momentum or you will have negative momentum. Both are forces that amplify what you are doing or what you are not doing. You will find that the moment you get yourself into motion; over time, you will develop the momentum that basically gets everything done for you.

Napoleon Hill said: "When the idea was first planted in my mind by Mr Carnegie, it was coaxed, nursed, and enticed to remain alive. Gradually, the idea became a giant under its own power, and it coaxed, nursed, and drove me.

Ideas are like that. First, you give life and action and guidance to ideas, then they take on a power of their own and sweep aside all opposition. Ideas are intangible forces, but they have more power than the physical brains that give birth to them. They have the power to live on after the brain that creates them has returned to dust."

What you want to do will require you to want it badly enough for it to impose discipline on you in order for you to act in harmony with its achievement. Over time it will gather momentum, and it will do everything for you from that moment on.

The price you must pay is in action, no matter how small, no matter how many people may criticize or laugh at you for doing so; it doesn't matter, you are committing to process. I can guarantee that the laws are exact, you do reap what you sow.

For a long time, you will not see it, but over time you will, and worrying about the time it will take to get there is pointless because as we all know, that the time will pass anyway!

Chapter 14

VISION

Being able to See in the Dark.

"Don't let others tell you what you can't do. Don't let the limitations of others limit your vision. If you can remove your self-doubt and believe in yourself, you can achieve what you never thought possible."
- Roy T. Bennett

XIV

I touched on the subject of vision in the previous chapter, but I felt that I needed to dedicate a chapter on this topic to add further clarity on a very important subject.

In the story of Moses and the Israelites, we are told that the Israelites were slaves in Egypt and that Moses, following God's commands, would lead them to freedom. What followed was a story of miraculous acts performed by God, forcing Pharaoh to free the slaves.

They left Egypt fueled by dreams of "the promised land", and they eventually ended up in the desert. Twelve spies were sent to do a survey of the new land for 40 days. Ten of them gave a negative report of the land (despite them actually agreeing the land was indeed the land of "milk and honey").

They claimed to have seen giants in the land and out of fear they decided that they could not take over the land.

They came back and spread the negativity amongst everybody, and as a result, God punished them for their lack of faith because this was obviously contrary to the promise He had made to them.

Their punishment was that they were to wander around the desert for forty years (a year for each day they did the survey). During this time, they murmured and complained.

Mentally and spiritually, many lost their way. They even ended up creating an idol of a false god in the desert, forcing God to create the ten commandments, and the idol was destroyed. Many of those, including Moses that started the journey died out in the desert, never seeing the "promised land". It was the ones who kept the faith and were obedient to the vision who made it to the promised land.

What makes this story fascinating for me is this:

Moses, according to the text, was said to be someone who was not good with words yet convinced an entire people to mobilize and leave Egypt. The number of Jews in Egypt, according to my research, numbered in the millions. Moses left Egypt with them having no idea where he was going; he basically led them with blind faith.

The journey according to scholars was only supposed to take 11 days (the distance from Horeb/Sinai to Kadesh in Cannan), yet it took them 40 years.

God seemingly had to erase the memories of the slavery in Egypt and had to let the old generations who harboured disbelief to die off in the desert. The nation had to undergo a process of unlearning in the desert; otherwise, they were simply going to transfer what they had still known in Egypt to the Land of Canaan (the promised land). Fear mixed with hesitation was instilled in them following the survey of the land, and that was what further created obstacles for them, adding to their time in the desert.

Your vision based on your great desire for your life is going to uproot you from your current life, and this is something you should expect. Your vision will be linked to something that is close to your heart (subconscious mind) that your life keeps bringing you back to in order that you may add your contribution in a bid to solve the problem. Whatever you experience in life that keeps irritating you at a passionate level is your duty to solve.

YOUR GIFTS

I believe every one of us was sent here endowed with a certain level of gifting. There are things that you are naturally good at doing that activate a sense of natural curiosity on your part. You are a seedling sent here possessing a reality buried within you. These gifts lie dormant in you awaiting the day you decide to recognize, accept, cultivate and manifest them.

I want you to know the world is not looking for you as a person, the world is looking for the gifts, creativity, and talents you are secretly harbouring. If you don't manifest yourself and what you are desperately trying to contribute to the world; the world will ignore you.

Those that do not accept this truth will be forced to live life under the roles imposed onto them by society. If you don't produce or express anything, all you can be proud of is what you consume.

You have to allow yourself to discover the gifts that reside within you for those are your direct ticket to everything you've ever wanted.

Many think that what they are carrying is insignificant or outside of them, out there in the world and so they never take what they have seriously or spend their whole lives looking everywhere else but within themselves.

The process is not as magical as most people make it out to be, it really is just being able to find that one thing that you can't stop thinking about and that you are already doing in a small insignificant way and take it seriously.

What you are going to eventually manifest with your vision, you already are right now just in a lesser form. The next level of your life is not foreign to your current level where you find yourself; instead, it is an escalation of a process that was already in motion over the many years of your life. Somewhat of a natural domino effect.

ADVERSITY

In the story of the Israelites above, they complained as they met with adversity. It is hard having abandoned everything you have ever known, being in a hot desert, starving and always being thirsty; they also had to see people die along the way. Nomadic life in the desert is not easy.

Understandably, many people get despondent. Adversity is a reality. You will be faced with adversity over and over again; you will be met with temporary defeat over and over again. You will hear the word "No" over and over again, so expect it.
What I want you to know, however, is that this is normal and not unique to you.

I have heard so many "No's" on my journey and only a few "Yes's", but the few "Yes's" were all I needed. All you need is one or a few "Yes's" in a plethora of "No's".

If you are not hearing any "No's", you probably aren't hearing any "Yes's" either because it means you aren't acting or reaching out to people enough. Hearing the word "No" will become a sound of success making its way to you because you are reaching out and opening yourself up to the possibilities! "Yes" will be a sound of success because you have reached out and have something of value to offer that someone needs, and it will confirm the steady movement forward. When you hear "No", keep moving forward without ceasing!

I don't know why it is designed this way, but it is almost as if you have to be tested for what you want, and it is adversity that builds character which is similar to building up one's muscles using weight training. Success does very little to build character.

So, treat adversity as something you will encounter but make sure you hold onto your vision and never lose sight of it. If you do, you lose!

Remember that "every adversity carries with it, the seed of an equal or a greater benefit", as Napoleon Hill said. The adversity, or the "No" you receive, is preparing for you for an even greater win. All you have to do is hold on!

I have seen this in my own life; my business had so many deals that went south, so many meetings with many promises that proved to be worthless. I wrote two completely different drafts of this book and then threw them out and started with a blank page (one got rejected and the other I felt did not come from a good place).

Looking back I can say that I am grateful for LITERALLY everything that I went through; every heartbreak, every failure and every time where I felt that this was it because I now understand exactly why I had to go through it.

Steve Jobs said:

"You can't connect the dots looking forward; you can only connect them looking backwards. So you have to trust that the dots will somehow connect in your future. You have to trust in something - your gut, destiny, life, karma, whatever. This approach has never let me down, and it has made all the difference in my life."

Everything is preparing you for what you asked for, and even as I'm typing this to you, I am being met with adversity from many different angles in some of my companies and clients. But this is all part of the process, and this process cannot be cheated. There are no shortcuts to fully manifesting yourself.

Adversity in itself stretches you and forces you to act in new ways that you never thought of acting, and this is ok. Feel it... But never let it cripple you; make sure you keep acting, for action is the ONLY antidote there is.

It will take as long as it takes for your mindset to change, and you will see as you improve, your environment will then change to match that improvement. Keep the faith!

ACTIVE FAITH

Something you're going to have to maintain throughout the journey is active Faith, and when I say active Faith, I mean continuous Faith. A force that keeps moving you into consistent action no matter how small. This is why I have to reiterate the fact that you really must be sure that what you've chosen to want, you really want.

Faith is: The substance of things hoped for and evidence of things not seen.

In simple terms, Faith is being able to see in the dark. Seeing in the dark is something that is crucial to this process of personal success.

Without that killer instinct and obsession with what you want, you won't generate the necessary energy and endurance to accomplish that which you want. My hope for you is that you use what you find within yourself to not only make you a lot of money but that you use it to contribute something special in the world and thereby pass it forward.

If you hold onto your Faith, you will find that you get random hunches and random ideas to do something.

YOU MUST FOLLOW EVERY HUNCH! One must enter action with boldness because hesitation only creates obstacles which is what Robert Greene speaks about as his 28th law in his book: "The 48 laws of power."

This is the power of your inner force, leading you in the direction you truly want to go. If you know the story of Hansel and Gretel and the bread crumbs, I want to say that the bread crumbs are there, but they are not discernable to your five senses and reason. Remember what Steve Jobs said about hoping that the dots connect going forward. You must let go of that which is deemed to be logical and rational because rationality is suicide to that part of you that believes in all things.

You know that you've unlocked your vision when you can see beyond where you are, and the view scares and excites you simultaneously. Your vision will not keep you where you are in comfort; you must be willing to continually expand beyond where you are because that is what the successful life is about (progressive realization). Constant growth is what it is about because if you are not growing, you are dying; if you are not improving, you are regressing.

Be around things that inspire your vision, so don't be afraid to start visiting expensive car dealerships, start having coffee at expensive hotels and start believing in things you aren't readily able to pay for. That feeling of insecurity is the feeling that will cause you to act in ways that are in line with that which you want.

Chapter 15

UNIVERSAL LAW

you start seeing it everywhere...

"There is a thinking stuff from which all things are made, and which, in its original state, permeates, penetrates, and fills the interspaces of the universe. A thought, in this substance, produces the thing that is imaged by the thought.

Man can form things in his thought, and, by impressing his thought upon formless substance, can cause the thing he thinks about to be created."
- Wallace D. Wattles

XV

Let us start with understanding the fundamentals of the Universal Law. We all believe in something; religion or a higher power. Some believe in nothing - atheists, nihilists... Hell, (excuse the pun) even believing in nothing itself is a belief in something.

I want you to keep an open mind and substitute whatever words I might use to describe the "force," the "universe,' the law of attraction or "God' with whatever word or name makes you comfortable.

My aim in this chapter is to activate whatever your belief system is and make you aware of how it works.

Throughout my journey, I have seen things happen in my life that I cannot explain. Call it miracles, wonders, an act of God, voodoo, or whatever you want to call it.

Random, inexplicable events have happened in my life, especially at the worst of times; just when I thought all was lost, the impossible happened but looking back now I can say it is because I fully believed in a result.

I felt as if there was a power or a force that was working with me, wanting me to acknowledge its existence. For many years I could only draw on this power when I was desperate, and that's when it responded.

Over the last decade, in my studies of self-mastery and success, I was made more aware of this power. I noticed that famous thinkers over the years were also aware of this power, and they called it by different names. I curiously dove deeper.

Ralph Waldo Emerson said: "Everything in nature contains all the powers of nature. Everything is made of one hidden stuff."

Look around you, what do you see, apart from this book? You see objects; you see a world. You see what you describe as reality, but when we consider that all you see and call "real", what do we mean? Is it real because we can see, smell, touch, taste and hear it?

If that's the case, then reality is what we perceive with our five senses. What about the sounds that dogs can hear, but we humans can't; if the dog can hear it, but we can't, does it then mean the sound does not exist?

We definitely cannot conclude this, and this then applies to all the other senses that we share with other animals who have a higher prowess with the senses than we do. Some colours exist that we can't even see. There are indeed levels.

The point I'm trying to make here is that there is more to that which we call Life than what we can perceive. Just as there are levels in the physical plane, there are also levels in the mental plane (grade

1 mathematics vs university-level mathematics). Then there are the levels on a spiritual plane. We will focus on the spiritual plane for this chapter.

We are all a part of everything; we are all made of the same "hidden stuff", and we all originate from that same "hidden stuff".

If you think about it now, there were moments in your life where you could sense something was off, but you were not sure. Later it was revealed that your feeling was correct. You could sense that someone was betraying you or lying to you, and it was indeed so.

Many people call this "intuition" or the sixth sense, but: intuition" simply means to learn from within, but we can go with the sixth sense for now.

What you experienced was a power within you that is connected to all things, to all knowledge and to all possibilities, it knows all, is all and creates all. We've often heard of the term "trust your gut" or "I have a hunch." These are all terms that we have heard, but because of their over-use, we have discounted their validity.

THE POWER

We are taught that this strange power exists outside of us, that it resides somewhere in the sky or some holy place; the truth, however, is that the power resides within us.
To drive the point home even further, THE POWER IS IN YOU.
It must then work through you, for you and manifest itself AS YOU!

The idea for Lohocla was just an idea. So how on earth did it become a real thing years later? How did I find all the right people at the right time who had EXACTLY what I needed at the time?

Did I make Lohocla all by myself? No. But somehow, a series of events and people were brought to me through channels I couldn't even begin to explain. Investors from thousands of miles away heard of what we were doing and decided to invest. This happened just as I had exhausted all known investment possibilities! The right amount, the right people, the right time. All this came together for the perfect solution. How did this all happen? Was it me? Hell no!

After experiencing this and reflecting on it, I came to better understand how this power works and how it is activated.

Jesus said something a number of times in similar ways, and I missed it when I was a churchgoer. See for yourself.

"Then Jesus said to the centurion, "Go! As you have believed, so will it be done for you." And his servant was healed at that very hour." Matthew 8:13

"So will it be done for you" means that you do not do it yourself, you will experience it, but it is not you doing it. Jesus is telling us that reality somehow mimics the beliefs that you hold.

I saw with Lohocla that when I was focusing on looking for the perfect bottle, all my focus went there and all that was brought to me was exactly what I needed.

This happened at every turn. You will also see this when you buy an item or maybe a car. As soon as you start looking for something specific, YOU START SEEING IT EVERYWHERE! It is all about what you turn your awareness to, that you grant focus to that you must ultimately create.

The beliefs you hold are the very things you must experience, and the power that resides within you does all that it can to make sure you attract experiences, people, and circumstances that corroborate with your beliefs. This is why people who never update their belief systems are forced to live under the very same conditions over and over again, like a scratch on a CD.

The power will give you anything you believe in; it is almost as if the power is a waiter in a restaurant called Life. The waiter presents us with the menu, and we pay for what we choose with our belief system.

The power can grant you anything you believe in because the chef of the restaurant has no idea who's ordering what. All the chef knows is that he or she must create the "food" the waiter has asked for on our behalf.

This is why it doesn't matter who you are, where you are, what colour you are, what you've been through, and how many failures you have previously encountered. The waiter does not care about all that; believe and order what you WANT from the restaurant of Life.

IT IS DONE UNTO YOU AS YOU BELIEVE.

This is how the power operates, and I want you to repeat this saying to yourself daily until it sinks in.

This means that poverty and wealth are nothing more than belief systems manifested, so is health and so is virtually everything else.

We've all heard of the Placebo Effect, how sugar pills can make patients think they are improving in health. This is all because of the power and how it operates.

This power will work for you the moment you acknowledge it and understand the laws in which it operates. It's all about your own belief system. All the greats we know in history understood this law and used it for their own purposes.

I also want to reiterate the fact that the power doesn't need for you to be aware of it, for it to work for you, it operates on law (that cannot be averted). Many people will see that they've used the power their whole lives without being aware of it. Today I want you to be mindful of it and actively work with it from this day forward.

This has been kept from society all of these years. Every single system of oppression has worked to conceal knowledge as well as control the belief system of a population, forcing them to continue to create a pre-programmed reality.

Whatever a population believes in at a macro level, it will continue to experience, but the power is always there to give them exactly what they believe in.

You are the creator of your own life experiences, and there is nothing that you cannot be or do provided you believe you can. You cannot live below the limits of your own belief system and so hope to occupy a higher plane of existence; you must begin by altering and updating your own belief system. You do this via the process of repetition I explained in chapter twelve, where we explored habits and subconscious programming.

IT IS DONE UNTO YOU AS YOU BELIEVE.

ENERGY

We are all a part of a system. We are not separate from it and just because we can identify ourselves from everything else around us, does not mean we all do not originate from the same place or hidden stuff. If you had to go lower and lower below the known properties of matter, below the sub-atomic level at the very core of everything, you would find that there is a single element or hidden stuff that from there forms everything at the higher levels.

We are all a part of one substance that is common to all of us. The separation between objects that are living and non-living is only from our perspective in a way that allows us to differentiate from types of matter.

You are not a drop of water (consciousness) in an ocean; no! What you are is an entire ocean (Life) contained in a single drop of water (consciousness). You possess all the qualities of the ocean of life in a smaller form. Once you remove your concept of separation and connect yourself to everything, you will find that you are all things and all things are you. This is a vast concept to devour, but the fundamentals I want you to take away for purposes of this book is that we are all connected somehow, and we are all a part of one substance that is inherent in all of us and flows through us all. Some have access to more of it; some have access to less of it. We will call that - Energy, and that's what I want your mind to hold onto.

IMAGINATION

Albert Einstein once said: "Logic will get you from A to B. Imagination will take you everywhere."

This above statement has become something that I now wholeheartedly live by. Logic in itself, while powerful, is limited because it can only operate based on what is behind it. Logic can't operate based on what's ahead of it because it can't see that far.

Whenever someone has told me something I wanted to do wouldn't work, I knew that they were operating from a perspective of what they knew (not to say they were wrong), but they didn't see what I could see because imagination allows one to see forward. Arnold Schopenhauer said that talent hits a target that other people cannot hit, but genius hits a target that people cannot see!

To transcend the limitations imposed on you, you are going to have to make use of the imagination. This is the workshop of the future, the place where all ideas originate from; the formless. Imagination by very nature predates reality.

Before you get dressed, you imagine what your clothes will look like on you, and then you get dressed. Before you go anywhere new, you imagine what it would be like even though most of the time it doesn't shape up the same, but the same use applies.

People use their imagination for small menial tasks but what I want you to know right now, is that your imagination is the very place where your new life will come from.

When I mentioned earlier regarding thinking yourself into a new reality and thinking yourself into a higher state of being, I was alluding to the fact that the imagination is the tool that will be used for this.

The vision for your life awaits you in your own imagination. This part of us was educated out of us by the school system but is the power that you must unearth. We all have the capability to be creative because all creativity springs forth from the imagination and is thus lying dormant in us all.

The universal laws seem to respond to the imagination; I now accept the fact that all thoughts are Energy, and they indeed produce a corresponding feeling or emotion that produces a reality that must ultimately be experienced.

Isaac Newton said that every action has an equal, similar and opposite reaction; thoughts held in imagination for long enough become things once acted upon. What things those are, only you will be able to readily identify, this is why it is very crucial that you become aware of the power of your thoughts and the power of the imagination.

Once you learn to yield to the imagination, you will see the power assisting you at every corner to accomplish that which you want to accomplish. With your imagination, you produce thoughts that pull to you, through the unseen sea of energy, all corresponding events that support your own conclusion that is held by your beliefs.

The power will move you into action so you can receive the very thing that you have knowingly or unknowingly asked for because every action must produce its very own corresponding reaction. You will feel or have a thought to do something that you can't shake. This is similar to falling for someone and having a voice in your head that prompts you to call or text the person which you either do or don't listen to.

SYNCHRONICITY

Synchronicity is a concept that was coined by the analytical psychologist, Carl Jung (1875-1961). Another word we could substitute for synchronicity is the word "serendipity". These terms simply mean the encountering of meaningful coincidences.

Almost like the universe at large, is winking and nodding at you to let you know that you're on the right path. The thing about meaningful coincidences is, you must be prepared to see them.

Once you've asked for something and you have followed all the other steps mentioned so far, the synchronicity happens as a sign to show you that the receiving is in process.

The problem is that we have been taught to believe that coincidences are meaningless and should be treated as random events. The word "coincidence" in English refers to circumstances without apparent causal connection, but when you unpack the same word in Hebrew it speaks to harmony, symmetry and coordination in circumstances, i.e. CAUSAL CONNECTION. The English language has watered down the meaning of the word drastically, and as a result of this, you have ignored many powerful signs your whole life.

From this day forward, I want you to get away from that sort of thinking and start being aware of life and how much of it is communicating with you on a daily basis. You now know that we are all connected. When you start accepting this way of life, you will start seeing synchronicities in every aspect of your life.

I've bumped into the very people I wanted to meet, I've had instances when I thought of someone, and they called or texted me soon after. Ridiculously, many of us have been asleep to life, our environment and its possibilities and suffered unnecessarily as a consequence.

When you accept that you are part of everything, when you want something or desire something, you must now know that you are putting a chain of events in motion that you must inevitably meet. Provided you stay long enough with what you've asked for, imagined, put into thought and performed the corresponding actions, you will receive. All desires are easily expressed in words or conversation, but all expectations are closely related to behaviour!

Be someone who from this day forward becomes a person who is expectant of the things they want. Life is not what happens to you. Life is what happens because of you. Don't ignore the signs.

The law states:

"Ask and you shall receive.
Seek and you shall find.
Knock and the door shall be opened unto you."

The power is alive and is active.
The power is working for you and working through you.

The power operates on one simple law:

IT IS DONE UNTO YOU AS YOU BELIEVE.

Chapter 16

MONEY MASTERY

From this day look at Money as a Tool to be Mastered

"WHATEVER may be said in praise of poverty, the fact remains that it is not possible to live a really complete or successful life unless one is rich. No one can rise to their greatest possible height in talent or soul development unless they have plenty of money; for to unfold the soul and to develop talent one must have many things to use, and one cannot have these things unless they have money to buy them with.

One develops in mind, soul, and body by making use of things, and society is so organised that man must have money in order to become the possessor of things; therefore, the basis of all advancement for humankind must be the science of getting rich."
- Wallace D. Wattles

XVI

MONEY AS A CONCEPT

Money, regardless of what might be said or thought about it, has immense power that one must respect. Money has the power to get people's attention; which is also why I kept this chapter for now. Everything has been building up to this chapter.

Money means many things to many people, to some, it's a healthy topic, and to others, it is a taboo or secret topic. Whatever the case, we all have some sort of relationship with money and that relationship determines a great deal of how we view life.

The concept of money is simply a medium of exchange. A tool that helps facilitate trading with each other in an easy way without the need for the old system of bartering.

This chapter will explore how one can master money. Money is a wonderful servant, but a terrible master, this is why I have had to wait until now to be able to divulge what I plan to reveal on this subject.

Money is a very important and touchy subject but one that you need today, to make a decision to become a master of. Only then will you be able to live out the full potential of your dream life and only then can you become the person you desperately want to be.

From this day look at money as a tool to be mastered and nothing else.

MONEY AND BELIEFS

In the previous chapter, we looked at how nobody can live beyond the limits of their own belief system. We also looked at how the unseen universal power is activated by belief. We internalised the Universal Law and summarised its way of operation in one line: It is done unto you as you believe. This wisdom applies to money too.

Most people inherit their relationship with money from their parents or the immediate environment that they grew up in. This dictates for them, going forward what money is and how they will relate it to it and what they believe about it.

These programmed beliefs will either be one of lack (fear-based) or one of abundance (love-based.)

If you were born into a poor or middle-class family, chances are you look at money from a perspective of lack; something that there isn't much of and that ought to be spent sparingly. Money was something that your parents were scared of running out of.

You would have seen your parents leave, day in day out, to go to work come back tired and as a result, formed their own relationship with money that was unknowingly projected in a state of stress. You were taught you must prepare your whole life by getting the best marks at school in order to secure the best stable job that guarantees the highest paying income. Because of this, you were then brought up under this belief system. This form of programming would have tainted your relationship with money. To thrive, you would have needed to update that belief system, sadly most people never did.

I came from a somewhat upper-middle-class family, and even so, I was programmed to associate with money from the perspective of lack. Money was something that was a limited resource, something to be used cautiously.

When I was young, I remember not being able to understand why it had to be so. One thing though, while my parents always made sure I had the best of everything, they also taught me how to wait for things by instilling delayed gratification into me. I am not sure if they were intentional about this or not, but it was a very good practice.

I never received an outright "no" for most things, but I was encouraged and taught to work for things. I was rewarded when I presented my report card, and so I didn't associate with lack but more a patient association with the things that I wanted.

I always knew I demanded a lot from life, and I think my parents could pick that up from a young age because I always had a funny way of making money even though it wasn't my intention. I just knew how to speak about things in such a way that would make the other kids want what I had for sale. I would test them by telling them it would cost a certain amount of money. I didn't expect any of them to follow through on it until the one day I sold a bunch of marbles to a kid for almost 1000% profit. I took the profit back to my mom, who wondered which 8-year-old kid had that much money to spend on marbles. Turned out that the kid had stolen the money from his parents and we had to drive out to their house that evening to return the money to them. Interesting story, looking back now, I shouldn't have given the money to my mom! I was not the one who had done something wrong.

I don't ever recall money ever being a limitation for me. While my parents were cautious with money, they somehow prevented me from seeing money as a limiting factor. I will forever be grateful to them for that. This is the programmed perspective that a child who grows up in a rich or wealthy family receives as they grow up.

Children don't learn by words; they learn by emulation - osmosis.

In general children of wealthy people see their parents interacting with people who have more time (wealthy people value time more) and overhear more positive conversations about money. These children learn to be comfortable talking up to authority at an early age (children from poor backgrounds fear authority figures). They experience the best money has to offer and never have a belief pattern of lack. They then develop extremely high self-esteem naturally or at least one better than that their lack-based counterparts. From a very early age, they are sent to the best schools that place them around children from similar backgrounds who have somewhat of a similar belief system regarding money that they hold.

What I'm trying to highlight here is that the children who are brought up in a lack-based perspective regarding money, not only make poor decisions unconsciously, but life automatically puts them in an environment that further solidifies that belief system as they grow up.

Children that are brought up in wealthy families who are brought up in an abundance-based perspective regarding money, not only make rich decisions unconsciously but life automatically puts them in an environment that further solidifies that belief system as they grow up.

What is even more frightening, is how life seems to keep people there not because this is what life does, but belief systems stick and are very hard to shake off. And so even if a child from a poor background makes a few rich decisions, he most likely still will stay poor to a large extent unless he completely alters his belief system. Conversely, if a kid from a wealthy background makes a few poor decisions, he will still stay rich to a large extent unless he completely alters his belief system.

Common statements people, parents and society make also serve a basis for why most people possess a lack-based relationship with money.

Statements like:

"Money is the root of all evil."
"Save for a rainy day."
"Money doesn't grow on trees."
"Rich people are greedy."
"Money comes from hard work."
"Money is evil."
"Money goes out faster than it comes in."
"It is a sin to have a lot of money."
"Rich people aren't happy."
"Only crazy people make a lot of money."
"We can't afford that."
"I am a struggling artist."
"Making money isn't easy."
"I hate bills."
"They don't pay me enough at work."
"I'm so broke."

"Life is hard."
"Dreams never come true, be realistic."
"Live in the real world."
"More money, more problems."

How many have you heard from those close to you?
How many have you caught yourself saying?

The list goes on! These statements are repeated so much in the news and society that they stick in the subconscious mind forcing one to act in line with these beliefs. These beliefs then unknowingly activate the universal law that gives one EXACTLY what they believe.

This is where most people in society find themselves when it comes to money and is the reason why the fear of poverty is the single greatest fear that rules humanity.

The first part of money mastery is to be aware of your personal and internal money constitution that you've knowingly and unknowingly adopted and face it for what it is.

If this is something you no longer want, then you must make the decision to no longer want that for yourself. You need to do this right now. Right where you are... by making a repeated exclamation to yourself.

You don't change something by fighting against it. You change something by making an active decision against it. You do this by saying to yourself: "I no longer want this for my life" and you then leave it behind by making a conscious decision to adopt a new thinking pattern based on principles of repetition I mentioned in the chapter of subconscious programming.

You must consciously learn a new way to think before you can subconsciously master a new way to be.

I want you to be all that you can be so that you can make the impact you want to make in the world. To do this you're going to need money, and some of you are going to need lots of it! I have said it before - It is ok to want it.

This is the moment...right now... I want you to shout:

"I AM GOING TO BE WEALTHY!!"

Be totally unapologetic about this.

WEALTH CONSCIOUSNESS

Before you can work towards generating money, you must adopt a wealth consciousness, and this begins by changing your internal dialogue. This is the point where you can now add money affirmations to your list of previous affirmations.

Here are a few examples:

"I make more money than I spend."

"Money flows to me effortlessly."

"I give people more in use-value, that what I take in cash-value."

"Being wealthy is my birthright."

"I make more than enough money for myself, and I am able to help the world and those I care about."
"I respect money and am thankful that I understand it."

"I am an abundant valuable human being, full of life and joy, and I attract opportunities, for my services for which I will claim in the form of money and continual increase."

You must write these down in words you can understand, and those that mean something to you. Take some time to write your affirmations now, and then commit to repeating them daily!

To further solidify the wealth consciousness, you are going to have to start increasing your level of exposure by exposing yourself to circumstances that instil a feeling of wealth in you. Remember that it's all about the feeling. Make it a habit to visit expensive places as I said before, even if all you can afford is a cup of coffee.
You want to get the feeling. This may seem weird at first; it did for me, but you have to provoke your own consciousness and force it to expand.

You can't strive for great wealth when you keep exposing your mind to smallness. I certainly do not mean that you must go on a spending craze, what I am saying is that you must be around wealth to quickly accustom yourself to it otherwise you will have a pretty misguided idea of what to aim for.

PRODUCING VALUE

In the story of my childhood that I shared at the beginning of this chapter, I highlighted the fact that I was able to sell marbles for over 1000% profit to another kid in my grade.

What was I doing here?

I didn't just sell him marbles; I sold him marbles that he deemed valuable after listening to my unknown sales pitch. The key here is the word: value.

To generate money into your life and lots of it, you're going to have to create some sort of value for people that they are willing to pay you for and you must get extremely excited and enthusiastic about what you have to offer. Money flows most to those that provide the most value in the form of service for others. People buy three commodities; products, services and knowledge. Your income at any level is determined by three things, according to Earl Nightingale:

1. The demand for what you have to offer.
2. Your ability to deliver or execute on your offering.
3. The difficulty of replacing you.

If you look at your income right now and look at what I have said above, you should be able to understand why your income is what it is. Or why you don't have any income. You should also know how to increase it.

YOUR GIFTS

The greatest way to generate great wealth is to discover your endowed gifts/talents and invest in them. Do this in such a way that by effectively using them, you are able to deliver to the world something that fulfils a need or a want. This becomes infinitely powerful when you are able to use your gifts to solve problems at mass. This book is an example of me creating value using a gift, that you or someone else can buy.

Myles Monroe used to say: "Where your gift comes into contact with a problem, the outcome is wealth."

The wealthiest people on the planet are those who serve the most people and solve the most problems. This makes the acquisition of money a very selfless act contrary to popular belief; it takes great courage to make money because it means backing yourself and putting yourself out there. Most people cannot handle this, and so they keep their gifts to themselves and stay hidden their whole lives all because of the fear of criticism once again.

Jim Rohn said: "Formal education will make you a living, but self-education will make you a fortune."

Racking up degree after degree, your whole life will never make you wealthy. I see many people do this; they think knowledge alone will bring them success. I understand it's because that's all they know. If you don't know you don't have to do something, you'll continue doing it.

Invest in yourself. Invest in your gifts. Invest in the things that you're naturally inclined towards and keep developing them in such a way that allows you to deliver value for others. That is how real money is made.

GETTING ORGANISED AND ACCEPTING RESPONSIBILITY

You might be in a good job right now, or an ok job or maybe you are in a dead-end career. Regardless of where you find yourself, you are going to start off now by accepting full responsibility for yourself by accepting that you got yourself where you are right now. And then you're going to start getting yourself organised in life, especially where your money is concerned. Order is the first law of heaven.

You are going to do one or both of these:

- Reduce your spending (especially on silly things)
- Augment your income (making it a point to increase your income by creating more value.)

I started by cutting out all the things I didn't need. I stopped shopping for years; I stopped going out and allocated EVERYTHING towards building my life as little as it was because I had no job and so I had to make every cent that I got count.

We all have to start somewhere, but you must work based on where you find yourself. If time is what you need, then you must stop wasting it on things that don't add to your future. I discovered that life will give you the tools to endure the process and not the tools to enjoy it. I did say before that the desert is only a temporary place, and one must never expect to thrive there!

Most are unaware of the tools that they have at their disposal, and these only become obvious to you the moment you shift your focus to look for opportunities. This makes what you choose to ignore, just as important as what you choose to focus on.

You will only see what you are ready to see. This process itself won't be easy, if it was, everybody would be doing it. Your vision will illuminate the possibilities to you. You will start by attracting resources in the form of people who can help and guide you along your path. (This is also why you must never be afraid to speak to as many people as you can about what you are doing...you just never know how they can help.)

People complain about not having time or money to invest in their vision or dream, yet they are totally oblivious to how much money and time they waste because they are out of control. Money seems to love order, and the more organised you are as a person within yourself and with what you wish to offer, the easier money seems to flow to you.

It isn't "more money more problems," it is rather, "more money, more responsibility."

You must expect more responsibility if you want to accumulate and have more money in circulation. I think that's also why companies are also called organisations.

As I went along on my journey, that the higher I wanted to go in terms of money, influence or power; the more responsibility I had to assume and get used to.

This will be the case in any field or endeavour you wish to become rich in. You will be paid and promoted according to your ability to handle responsibility and to manage the conflict that comes with any level. This is why you must commit yourself now to getting yourself under control and disciplined. It doesn't help that you apply these principles to get rich only to lose it all.

Your skills, talents and gifts will make way for you in this world and even get you paid, but it is your character that will either keep you there — or your lack of character that will ensure that you get exiled... So, decide now to get yourself under control, especially when it comes to your vices. Your level of wisdom determines your level of wealth.

MONEY AND ENERGY

In chapter 15, I said that we are all connected somehow. I said that we are all a part of one massive energy. I then said that there are people who have access to more energy than others because of their mindset.

If we are all a part of one energy, and money is about creating value for other people that they pay you for, it then means that money is just a flow or reallocation of energy; money itself is energy. When you can grasp this and understand that every action has an equal, similar and opposite reaction; you will see that you attract people, circumstances and events based on the level of energy you are projecting. This is why vision always attracts resources!

The moment you have created something of value for others, you are going to raise your energy by putting yourself out there in real life or digitally. When you raise your energy, you automatically must raise your bank account if you have built a system that allows money to come to you. This means you must have a product or service, you must have a bank account, a way to market what you have to offer and a way to deliver the product or service. Most people create or do things then proceed to hide those things from other people because they once again fear criticism.

You don't put a light under a table! When you shine your light and project it effectively with enthusiasm, you will gain attention which will make people aware of what you have to offer and those that are interested will pay you for it. It doesn't help that you create something and then gain no awareness for it. Obscurity will kill any chance of you making money.

This is why individuals and businesses need marketing. Marketing is used to ensure they are seen by the target audience, and this is all paid for using money (energy). Action reaction, cause and effect.

This concept also leads me to the crucial aspect of networking. I once read that your network determines your net worth, and I agree. You are only as effective as your network. The greater and more powerful your network, the more access to energy you have and the more channels you have to project the value you have to a wider audience. Powerful people aren't powerful because they have strength; they have power because they have access to a lot of money which in our case is energy. Companies like Apple, Facebook and Amazon are high energy companies and are thus powerful. This is true for the individuals that run these companies; they were able to focus their energy and create those companies.

The more hands you shake, the more money you will make.

COMPETITION

The western culture has driven this concept of competition into the world, which I now see is a terrible lie. The delivery of value cannot be limited to just one source or one organisation. If that were the case, then there would be one musician in each genre or one type of car or one type of food. The beautiful thing about life is variety and change; what people liked last year has changed dramatically this year.

I've heard of people's ideas shot down because someone, usually in the investment field, said there was too much competition in that field. The potential investor would use a limiting term like: "the market is saturated."

I want you to know that there is no such thing. Obviously, one has to administer some sort of intelligence when it comes to their business endeavours. It doesn't help to create ice cream and then hope to make it big selling it in the North Pole!

If you find a problem to solve that someone else is already solving, it doesn't mean this is a no go area. You can come up with your own unique way to deliver value or to solve the problem, and if you feel strongly enough about and allow yourself to get obsessed by it, it can still work because you will be able to find a niche (genius hits a target other people cannot see). If you believe wholeheartedly in what you are doing, you will automatically activate the universal power that will do it for you.

You must do it with the intention of wanting to provide your own form of value for a problem people are experiencing and not to do it to dethrone someone or something else. Doing so will cause you to operate on the premise of lack, and you will then operate on the laws of winning or losing.

I think we can agree that trying to dethrone Coca Cola as a company isn't going to happen and that in itself is not a wise thing to do, but if you want to create a new flavour they haven't thought of yet, you can do that and even get rich off of it because you will find people that are interested in it.

The whole idea of competition assumes that your win is someone else's loss, and that's why the world constantly finds itself in a jam much of the time. You are going to create and not compete, and you are not going to accept what negative people tell you regarding saturated markets because that which resides within you is new in nature and thus seeks a new expression or incarnation through you.

Don't be afraid to talk to as many people about your ideas as possible. Most people are afraid to do this for fear of being judged, but they are also afraid of people stealing their ideas.

Know that even if people do steal your ideas, they cannot steal your execution. Your execution of the idea is based on your own unique, authentic conviction.

It takes a tremendous amount of work to internally change one's life, and most people are too afraid to pursue their own ideas or inclinations. Understanding that, how will they steal your ideas and execute on them when the idea came from you about a problem you are passionate about?

So, talk to as many people as you can about what you are doing or want to do. People are there to help you. The woman in my life once told me that "People are Gods' own hands" which makes sense if we are all one, I do thank her for that!

MULTIPLE STREAMS OF INCOME

I have yet to come across an extremely wealthy person who doesn't have multiple streams of income. There really is no specific number that you should aim for, but as I said before, you just have to follow your efforts.

We are all multi-dimensional beings, and the fun part about making money is the creation of new combinations that we form from our own unique perspectives that we form in relation to reality.

That's how it goes, you don't need some money expert to help you make these decisions unless you really want to, but one rule of thumb is that you never get into something unless you possess an in-depth understanding of it.

People over-complicate the process. It should be fun because all it is, is you expressing yourself to the world and sharing your creativity with others.

I must repeat this; YOU MUST FOLLOW YOUR EFFORTS.

Following your passions is a "kumbaya" saying and that holds no weight if a person puts no effort in their passions; if your passions and efforts are aligned, then you've hit the jackpot because you won't feel like you're working. That's exactly how I felt while writing this book.

To get rich you must invest in one thing. Putting all of your eggs in one basket, a basket you wholeheartedly believe in, and have a level of gifting/understanding in (my assumption here is that you don't have all the money in the world and so you have to be wise with how you use it).

Once you are rich, in order to stay rich, you then diversify. The concept of "spray and pray" in the beginning is a losing formula. It's all about focusing energy, a perfect example of this is a magnifying glass; you don't burn anything by constantly moving it around.

Focus on one thing and then once that thing becomes a success, you use the momentum of that success and who you have become to build the next thing. You will see that once you gain the consciousness of success, you never really start from the bottom of anything you wish to do.

It's also not about hoarding money but letting money work for you since it is a tool; a tool is useless when it is sitting around doing nothing. Money must always be in circulation. When you start making money and lots of it; let it work for you by spreading it around. Stuart Wilde once said: "Money is like fertiliser, if you pile it up, it stinks, but if you spread it around, it makes things grow."

Note that I in no way promote irresponsible behaviour - discipline must apply always!

MONEY PHILOSOPHY

Before we wrap up this chapter and Part 2 as a whole, I want to say that what you have learnt is a new way to be. This comes with a new philosophy that is powerful enough for you to use to make an impact in your world. I hope you do!

You must decide what your philosophy is going to be moving forward regarding money and to keep improving it as you go.

It is about making changes in a way that you're comfortable with. Decide how much money you're going to make and write it down, decide what kind of relationship you want with money going forward, and manifest it like any other desire you wish to manifest; money works on similar principles.

There is nothing that you cannot be, do or have; if you believe in it wholeheartedly, you can achieve it! What you hold in imagination, you can hold in your hands.

Aim for the highest expression of who you are, and always remember that money is a tool that facilitates that process.

Everything people have said to you regarding money is something that must now be in the past, who you were is no longer applicable. You are going to have to be comfortable with letting go of the old version of you in order for you to give birth to the new, more powerful you that must come into existence.

People will be forced to change the narrative that they have held of you, and once again, money will facilitate this process. Remember, all money does is amplify what you already are, and I hope you use this knowledge to do good in the world because the world certainly needs it.

Money buys time, and time leads to choices, and those choices lead to freedom. So, hold freedom in all forms as your highest priority and use that time to not only make a massive impact in your environment but to help you spend time with the people you love and care about while making positive changes in their lives. Build a life that you enjoy, don't spend years building a life you don't enjoy!

You will become more valuable to those that you love when you become powerful.

Please be very aware that this chapter was just a summary, and there are many books that go deeper into the topic of money, sales generation, investing tools etc. (see my recommended reading list at the back of the book)

I chose to focus on the main principles - the basics that are timeless; it is now on you to go further than where I've taken you to form the philosophy you want to develop around money and life.

PART THREE

RE-LEARNING

Chapter 17

ATTITUDE

Wisdom is Knowledge plus Reflection.

"The greatest revelation in my generation is the discovery that human beings, by a change of inner attitude can produce outer changes in harmony with their inner convictions."
- William James

XVII

It is often said that our attitude towards life determines life's attitude towards us. This re-enforces what I have said: life is what happens because of us, versus being what happens to us.

Your attitude is a reflection and a result of your will and belief system. A person who adopts an attitude of not being able to do something, won't be able to do it, whereas a person who adopts an attitude of being able to do something will be able to do that very something; and this is an inexorable fact. I wish this were something I had understood when I was younger, but I'm glad I can give this to you today if you weren't already aware of it.

You are either going to assume a progressive attitude towards life, or you are going to adopt a regressive attitude towards life.

It is indeed a binary concept that then determines the rhythm of your life provided that you hold the right attitude. The wrong actions with the right attitude will eventually be turned into the right actions and produce yielding returns, whereas the right actions with the wrong attitude will eventually be turned into the wrong actions and eventually produce no yield. Attitude is everything!

AWARENESS

It is important you first become aware of your own attitude before anything else. Only when you become aware of your attitude towards life, will you, based on results, know where and how to tweak it to get even better results than what you currently are experiencing.

Wisdom is knowledge plus reflection.

Being able to self-introspect is crucial in being able to chart a new course; one must know where they are so that they can decide on where to go.

Facing yourself is probably one of the most difficult things you're ever going to have to do because it forces you to admit to yourself that you probably aren't good enough...YET. As harsh as it might be, the medicine of this admittance proves to be exactly what the patient (you) requires.

I think we are too soft on ourselves and being soft is ok if you don't want to be something. Soft is ok if you don't want to affect your world and if you are happy to sit in a dark corner somewhere hiding who you are and what you have.

If you want to be more than you currently are, you're going to have to be hard on yourself in order to expect more from yourself and improve from where you are. It is only when you improve that you find that the circumstances and conditions of your life tend to change and match that improvement. It all begins with being aware of where you are right now.

SELECTION

The moment you become aware of your attitude, it is imperative that you make intentional adjustments to ensure you assume a progressive mindset. Notice how I said that if you don't assume a progressive mindset, you automatically adopt a regressive mindset and this is because the unfed mind devours itself.

If you don't select your attitude, you automatically will operate on the base attitude society operates on, and that is a regressive and general negative attitude. Success or failure is predicated on this word "attitude" because it determines the world in which you live in.

People with a regressive mindset are those who expect to find more bad in the world than they find good. These people choose to believe life is tough, dull and something that has to be endured. They think that everything is out to get them and so they do all that they can to protect themselves. They believe in very little and lack confidence and purpose in whatever they do. When a person is like that, it is not long that they fall into altercations with almost everyone that they know. This regressive attitude never grants anyone a magnetic personality. Because of that, they never attract people (and we have spoken about the power of finding the right people in life).

People with a progressive attitude are people who expect more good in the world than they do bad. They expect to win more than they expect to lose!

They simultaneously understand that all losing is only temporary. These are the kind of people that seek to solve problems in the world.

They do not passively identify and admire problems - they solve them! These are the people that are in the field, playing the game, rather than sitting in the stands criticizing everything they see.

A progressive attitude is something that you will be attacked for having. This comes with the territory because people who have progressive attitudes believe in more, more than what is merely immediately before them. They live above circumstances and conditions because they understand that everything once again is temporary.

Select the attitude you wish to be ruled by, then work to dominate your entire being by it because you become your most dominant state of mind.

You must first assume the consciousness of the results you want before they harden into the material. For these very reasons, you will mentally live in sunny conditions, even if your circumstances are stormy.

Chapter 18

OPPORTUNITY

Opportunities don't just pop up out of nowhere

"The Chinese use two brush strokes to write the word 'crisis.' One brush stroke stands for danger; the other for opportunity. In a crisis, be aware of the danger - but recognize the opportunity."
- John F. Kennedy

XVIII

We often see people all around the world protesting on the streets to their governments demanding more or better opportunities. We've also often heard of stories of how people leave village towns to go to the cities for more opportunities.

I did a little digging into the word "opportunity" and found it originated from the Latin word "oppotunitas" which is made up of two other terms "ob" and "portus."

ob: toward
portus: port

The combination phrase "ob portus" was used by sailors who often encountered terrifying ocean conditions. Remember, these sailors had nothing like the technology we have today, and yet they faced the same wild seas we have today. The design and technology used in ocean-going vessels have massively improved - the sea is as wild as it was then - and yet, even today we have shipwrecks. The sailors were courageous souls.

This should put the word "ob portus" into perspective. It was used to denote the best conditions that a sailor would use in order to sail towards the port given the tide, wind and current.

This was only possible if the captain of the ship had an idea of the port or destination. This meant that the captain not only had to know of the weather conditions but also know where he was going; otherwise, it would all be useless.

Outside the harbour, the ship was in a constant state of "opportunitas" if the captain knew where to go, and how to get there.

The word opportunity today, according to the Cambridge dictionary, means "an occasion or situation that makes it possible to do something that you want to do or have to do or the possibility of doing something."

Today's modern definition only speaks of external circumstances that relate to opportunity, whereas the origin of the word included both the external as well as internal circumstances. This means the person who is in search of the opportunity must assume responsibility in order to be in a state of "oppotunitas" for him or her to claim the opportunity.

To redefine the word for purposes going forward: An opportunity in this regard then means not only an event that happens to you from the external but one that you've had to actively and intentionally move yourself towards.

PREPARATION

There is a process to best tackle opportunities with and, it starts with preparation.

Opportunities have always been grasped by those who are ready to grasp them. Some were aware of this process, others not. Those that were unaware of the process have not been awakened to how this same process applies to other aspects of life.

A college/university student will study for 3 or 4 years for a degree and then go forth and seek a job at companies that are operating in the vicinity or occupation that is closely matched to what he/she studied.

A soccer player would know to have practised, trained and played in order to develop the skills before approaching a soccer team to play professionally.

I had to first write this book before putting it in the hands of an editor and printers in order to get it published.

What have I highlighted here?

The secret to understanding opportunity lies in the grasping of the concept of preparation.

People protesting on the streets, begging for opportunities (even though possibly warranted) have missed the concept of preparation. They are mentally depending on people or institutions to give them some sort of assistance that they deem as "opportunity". Because of their understanding of opportunity in the old term, they will never receive what they fully want.

I have long come to the conclusion that the world is not in the business of handouts, and if it is, then it definitely does not have enough handouts to go around. This calls for a complete rethinking of the approach.

It took years of preparation to become aware of the opportunities that would turn Lohocla the product into what it is now.

I have not quite fully come to terms with what constitutes a person's awareness, but it seems to me that you must become so obsessed with wanting something and then, while moving towards your goal, train your mind to filter out everything unnecessary in your world, so you become incredibly focused on that which you are seeking.

If a person is hungry and filled with the feeling of hunger, their mind fills with thoughts of food which then filters out everything else and gives them all sorts of ideas for food, which we call "cravings." Once the person has eaten, their thoughts then may return to whatever it was they were thinking of before the hunger struck.

Opportunities don't just pop up out of nowhere and fall on your lap, and if that is how you think this is going to happen, you are completely delusional.

As soon as you decide on what you want and are completely fixed on it and subconsciously full of this desire, you will start to move towards this goal. This is why you will begin to have ideas or hunches. These ideas and intuitions are your mind filtering out the noise, allowing you to see all the routes that will take you where you want to go.

You always see in the world, what you are prepared to see, and this relates to opportunities too. The vision you hold for your life not only imposes self-discipline on you, but it simultaneously gives you new eyes that allow you to see all the opportunities that have been around you all this time.

LUCK

Luck is not some magical or miraculous occurrence but an inevitable consequence of the law of cause and effect. This explains why successful people create their own luck. Successful people assume a progressive attitude towards life and act accordingly in the state of preparation.

For them, preparation inevitably meets opportunity because, in their movement towards the goal, they are pursuing, it seems as if the possibilities avail themselves and the world just seems to hand itself over to them. I've seen this in my own life.

John Anster said: "The moment one definitely commits oneself, then providence moves too. All sorts of things occur to help one that would never otherwise have occurred. A whole stream of events issues from the decision which no man could have dreamed would have come his way. Whatever you can do, or dream you can do, begin it. Boldness has genius, power and magic in it. Begin it now!"

To the untrained eye, it is almost as if that person is constantly performing miracles. But once again, it is cause and effect, action-reaction or sowing and reaping. This is something you must be aware of.

Luck is:

an inevitable consequence of a person who relentlessly pursues an endeavour while constantly adapting their approach (preparation) - until their awareness is expanded, and they see all the doors they must walk through that are aligned to the vision they hold within their heart (opportunity).

Now you know what it means when people say he or she "is so lucky" when it comes to matters of achievement.

Chapter 19

RISK-TAKING

Without Risk, there can be
No substantial Reward

"If you are not willing to risk the unusual, you will have to settle for the ordinary." - Jim Rohn

XIX

If there is another thing that I have seen that holds people back, it has to be the concept of risk-taking. This has been instilled via the fear of poverty as well as the fear of criticism.

Fear forces people to be risk-averse and imagine all the reasons why something can't be done, and so they never even attempt to go after the things they want.

Without risk, there can be no substantial reward, and this comes once again from the law of sowing and reaping. You cannot expect to make withdrawals in life where you have not previously made deposits.

To achieve anything new in your life or to go to the next level of what you are currently doing, you are going to have to start acting in radically new ways. To achieve new results, you are going to have to assume some risk. Only a fool does the same things over and over and expects different results.

Taking risks opens you up to new possibilities that would never have availed themselves to you if you had not assumed the risk. Playing it safe limits your field of awareness and keeps it locked to new opportunities. Safety or comfort is not concerned with anything new; rather it is a state of mind that is concerned with holding onto what is known and only seeks slow, minimal and predictable growth in confides accepted by the majority.

The problem comes when people expect all these wonderful things to happen in their lives, yet they are so busy acting like everyone else. It is this concept of risk-taking that separates the people who make it big in the world versus the people who go nowhere.

EMBRACING RISK

People talk of "calculated risks", and this idea always made me question its validity. The whole concept of risk infers an element of blindness to the outcome, yet still expecting and acting in ways that affirm a positive conclusion. Assuming risk is not gambling.

People who bet on football games or horse races, for the most part, are gambling. The person who believes he can turn their passion love and effort of writing into income can do so if they maintain their vision and then act.

A person who backs themselves will find that the divorce of safety, even though uncomfortable at first, will transmute itself into greater returns in the long-term. Short term thinking, however, kills long-term results.

A conviction for your life will make you uncomfortable at first because you will be leaving everything you've known and held onto. For a higher order of life, this is the price that must be paid. Your new life will cost you your old life. As soon as a person becomes aware of the call and feels it, they can no longer deny it.

Risk-taking will put you in the playing field of your life where you are able to allow yourself to be exposed to the elements which will be scary at first.

I told myself that regardless of what I have to face in life, life has brought me here for a reason and as long as I accept the call of my life, it somehow must take care of me and whatever comes my way I should be able to handle.

This was my attitude towards all the risk I had assumed, especially when I was deep in debt.

It takes tremendous courage to assume risk, put yourself in debt, not knowing how you'll pay it back should your vision fail — all for a vision that you can feel but cannot physically see. I had to do this because remaining where I was, was more painful than risking everything for the possibility of a brighter future.

And this is what I want you to know right now. As long as you hold onto your vision and master the principles found in this book, success is guaranteed because your life is of massive importance to the grander scheme of things and the universal power seeks maximum expansion through you. You becoming more is in the best interest of everyone and everything.

And that's where I find myself today typing what you are reading now. I can say that all the risks I have taken over the years have paid off 100-fold. Life is not perfect, and I still continue the journey, but I am filled with excitement for every new moment.

It has taken up until now to mess up your life unconsciously, and I am by no means saying this is easy but know that it will take a fraction of those years to first actively repair your life, and then start living a brand new life that is closely tied to who you really are.

This entire movement will require you to embrace risk in all aspects of your life, and only you will know what risk means to you, but without taking the risk, you will never reap the reward.

This is not something I can sugarcoat even though I wish I could.

Chapter 20

PERSISTENCE

No matter how Sharp your Axe is, it is going to take Time

☥

"If you're going to try, go all the way. Otherwise, don't even start. This could mean losing girlfriends / boyfriends, wives, relatives and maybe even your mind. It could mean not eating for three or four days. It could mean freezing on a park bench. It could mean jail. It could mean derision. It could mean mockery--isolation. Isolation is the gift. All the others are a test of your endurance, of how much you really want to do it. And, you'll do it, despite rejection and the worst odds. And it will be better than anything else you can imagine. If you're going to try, go all the way. There is no other feeling like that. You will be alone with the gods, and the nights will flame with fire. You will ride life straight to perfect laughter. It's the only good fight there is."

– Charles Bukowski

Persistence is probably the most important success principle of all. I have written on many principles in this book that I fully live, but there is none more unavoidable than persistence. This is the principle that most people who never make it, fail at!

It is almost as if there is a force or power at work that allows nobody to win at something substantial unless they have proven they can be persistent even in the face of constant defeat over a long period of time.

We are here on a spiritual journey of refinement and evolution. Look at the process of how gold is extracted from ore. Gold is heated to ridiculous levels to remove impurities from it! It seems as if nature refuses to let anyone enjoy valuable and massive success without being refined through a rigorous process. It is through trials and tribulations that the character is refined to a point where a person can evolve to be worthy of the goal they seek.

I think everyone who has succeeded massively in any endeavour involving risk would be able to tell you of the many years of struggle and constant failures along the way that only made sense later on upon introspection when the win was apparent.

There have been many times in my life where I attempted the impossible. I had to maintain persistence. In business, this concept of persistence becomes even more apparent. Calling a person once or sending one email is not enough; people have a million other things on their minds, and you and your ideas don't matter to them. I learnt early on that some people were only willing to do something for me when they accepted that I wasn't going away because I'd call every single day if I had to. That is the level I accepted I had to operate from.

There were times where just as I was about to win; the rug would be pulled from under my feet. Whether it was someone changing their minds or an investor backing out of a deal; it hurt like hell, but I continued to persist.

I learnt early on that I preferred hearing a 'no' rather than not getting an answer because a "no" meant that that door was temporarily closed, and I could go forth and try something else. Over time you see a pattern; it doesn't get easier; you can just more readily identify with it more when it happens.

It is for this reason I've accepted that persistence ought to be mastered and not just learnt. This principle alone is the difference between success and failure. Most people who accept failure as a permanent result never get up from that not because they can't, but it takes everything to create the momentum required to create success.

PATIENCE

Regardless of how hungry you are for what you want, you have to accept that great things take time. There is always a gestation period between cause and effect. It takes a human baby nine months to form, and I think we can agree that no matter how excited both parents are for the baby, there is no way that baby will pop out complete and healthy after four months. And this is exactly how it will be for any massive and important endeavour you're going to pursue.

It is going to take time, firstly to work on yourself and then to do the work you wish to do in your effort to contribute to your world.

It is never easy to be patient, especially when you want something badly. Looking back now, I am grateful that I didn't get the things I wanted in the timeframe I first wanted them in. I only got them when I was ready to handle them because, in this world, your level of promotion will be directly linked to your ability to handle responsibility and manage conflict.

When I say patience, I also don't mean that you must be sitting back, waiting for things to happen because that sort of patience will kill you. You must be able to do all that you can do daily and when you can do no more, let go and let the universal power handle the rest. Everything you want is on the other side of not giving up!

TIME

If you are worried about the time it will take, remember that the time will pass anyway. In the grander scheme of things, time is a concept we humans created; the universe doesn't operate with concepts such as time and space. According to the universe, everything is in a state of now.

What gets people is only their perceived notion of time relative to their environmental pull. This is where the pressure comes from - from an unhealthy obsession with what other people are doing. For example: You somehow have to have your life figured out by 25, married by 30 and then kids and on and on. If you aren't married by 25, you feel a sense of failure...? Who set this standard of time, and why do you allow it to pin you down and control you?

You will unfold when you unfold, and you will become everything you've ever wanted in the time it takes YOU TO BE READY and not a moment sooner or later. Stop worrying about what other people think about you and what you should be achieving by whatever age and be sure that you think correctly about yourself.

MASSIVE ACTION

Winston Churchill said: "Success is the act of moving from failure to failure without a lack of enthusiasm," he definitely was talking about being persistent. He also went on to say: "If you're going through hell simply just keep going!"

In my journey to establish Lohocla, regardless of the years it took, I was still as obsessed with every fine detail of the product as I was in the beginning. I had not allowed all the years of rejection amidst the few yesses to slow me down and make me lose enthusiasm.

I carried this mindset through to when I decided to launch my own seminars and write this book. Action is the only thing I now understand, and I command, massive amounts of it!

You are going to have to be persistent with your actions in massive amounts. Persistence is something social media experts will stress to you, as well as personal trainers, athletes and any place where you wish to achieve highly. Yet, people refuse to accept this when it comes to success and their endeavours. The same principles pop up in countless fields.

If you have an axe and are planning to chop a big tree down, we can all agree that no matter how sharp your axe is, it is going to take time and it is going to take consistent and persistent actions in one spot. And this is precisely how you are going to approach whatever it is you wish to do or achieve.

You are going to select one thing, and you are going to hit at that one thing for however long it takes for it to become something worthwhile.

I had to learn this lesson the hard way by having many ideas I was trying to get out; little did I know I was just wasting energy by not focusing it (remember what I said about the magnifying glass). Only once you master something do you then move on to the next thing. Most people give up when they don't see results in a time frame that they expected things to happen for them.

It was my Dad who told me: "Your plans will always come to fruition provided you keep working at them but not in the timeline that you expect them to." I thought he was crazy when he said that, but I now accept that.

Without a doubt, I am where I am now because I was consistent with my actions. I was massively consistent with massive actions!

Exert a level of action in your endeavours that is greater than the environmental pull of mediocrity that is trying to bring you down.

All life falls under the concept of entropy which means that all things tend to revert to chaos if you don't keep them in order. A garden will become a bush if you don't tend to it.

Life becomes a lifestyle when you commit to being intentional about it by use of intentional amounts of action. Do this, and there is no going back.

SACRIFICES

When people are actively trying to change their lives, I have noticed that they start by adding new things rather than by eliminating things.

This is a failing formula. Your life is already filled to the maximum with routine; the problem is that many of them are not good habits or routines. Your life follows a pattern that is dominated by habit and those habits fill the space of your awareness.

So even if you consciously do something new today, there is a high chance that you will be pulled back to what you did yesterday. Although you are trying to do something new mentally, your body is run by a different program because a habit is formed when your body has learnt to do something better than what your mind can; it now becomes a part of your being. You need to create space for the new habit to take root.

SACRIFICES CREATE SPACE.

The concept of sacrifices is a process whereby one removes what is unnecessary for the journey in order for you to free up space. You can then reallocate energy to the entrenchment of the new progressive habits.

Sacrifices will be in the form of nights out, unnecessary spending, distancing yourself from friends who don't add to you, spending less time with family or maybe even ending a relationship.

This is what it takes to make a person more persistent. We can all agree that if you have a long-distance to walk, the less you carry, the greater your chances of arriving at your destination in a good and healthy condition. The fewer things holding you down, the more energy you have.

It can be more difficult to let go of things than it is to start new things, but it is this process of letting go of things or people that no longer serve you that will grant you the space to add new things that not only benefit you but that actually stick.

Making sacrifices for a higher life is something that comes with the territory that is unavoidable because your new life will indeed, cost you your old life. This is the price you must be willing to pay.

Not everyone can go with you on your journey to success, and only those that are committed to growth can go with you.

I can't make this any plainer or say it in a nicer way. This is hard, and this is real, and this is the blunt truth.

TEMPORARY DEFEAT

I've addressed failure already in chapter seven, but I must bring it up again. We are in the business of repetition because that's how the subconscious mind is reprogrammed.

On your journey, you will be met with countless amounts of defeat, rejection and failure.

This is normal.
This is temporary.
This is not unique to you!

You will have the air knocked out of you by a blow to the face, but you only lose when you quit. You will have to persist. Chances are you'll be hit more than once in the face. You have to get up, and the only thing that will force you to persist and get up is the strength of your desire and the intense pull of your vision.

Massive success works on a formula, and once you master its principles and allow yourself to fully gain the mindset of a winning attitude, there is a high chance you will never fail at anything in your life ever again, and if you do it won't hurt as bad.

Chapter 21

HEALTH

We are Multidimensional Beings

"To keep the body in good health is a duty… Otherwise, we shall not be able to keep our mind strong and clear."
- Buddha

XXI

We've covered the mental and spiritual aspects of life in much detail, but I now must emphasize the physical aspect.

We are multidimensional beings who occupy three spheres, mental, spiritual and physical. Self-mastery is about mastering, respecting and feeding all three spheres. Neglecting one will make the other two suffer. You must aim to be holistic.

I chose to focus on the physical least in this book because there is just so much out there already. Society seems obsessed with the physical nature of humanity. There is a lot of good stuff out there - go get it! I must briefly touch on a few things you already know.

The concept of health is such an important discussion because this is a topic people disregard until something drastic happens to them. Only then do they give it the necessary attention it requires. We very easily take things for granted and just because we got our body for free, we often take very little care of it.

I used to be a person that didn't take much active care of my body until I realized that this was no longer in line with the vision I had for my life.

I can't stand in front of people telling them how to transform their lives when I was not taking care of my body. You really can't take people somewhere you can't take yourself first.

I primarily want to stress that you must take care of your body. You don't need to be a person who gets called up for magazine covers, but you must know your body and keep it in the best possible condition. Don't focus too much on Hollywood bodies that are photoshopped before we see them.

Watch your diet - I am not just talking about being overweight - many slim people can also develop cholesterol and sugar problems from the things they eat and the way they live.

Take care of your health as early as possible; many health problems only show themselves years later.

You only have one body, and it doesn't matter how rich you become, or how enlightened you become; if your body is giving up on you then there really is no point to it all now is there?

My vision for my life demands the discipline of looking after my body. I want to live a long and healthy life. I want to contribute a tremendous amount to this planet by reaching billions, and for that, I'll need a body that is in the best working order so that it will work with me rather than against me.

EXERCISE

Make it a point to be active; take a walk 3 or 4 times a week, run, or sign up for gym. The aim is not to be this ripped athlete; the aim is for you to respect yourself enough to take care of yourself.

How you do and treat one aspect of your life, is how you do and treat everything else in your life because everything permeates into everything else and everything bleeds into everything else.

Be a complete human being walking around with your head held high as an example of what it truly means to be manifested. This world is starved for people who are in control of themselves.

You are going to have to become a person that takes care of their body; so do a bit of research into it and adapt your diet and exercise according to your requirements. Drink plenty of water.

There is no right or wrong, but you must do what works for you. If after additional research, you are still uncertain, then see a health professional, but make sure they are about true health and not just what looks good.

In this regard, all that matters to me is that you become a person with a health consciousness, and remember that everything must be done in moderation. Don't do too much too soon. Exercise gets easier over time and that automatically makes you want to exercise more.

You are developing a philosophy of being in control of yourself and not allowing yourself to get out of control in any aspect of your life; this grants you a state of calmness amidst chaos. Exercise is good for the mind!

You will be more valuable to yourself and to everyone you come into contact with, and this will greatly improve not only yourself but your family and loved ones.

Your vision for your life will require you to be full of energy, and it is this energy that will help you accomplish the things you wish to accomplish. If you are currently in a situation where you've allowed your body to wither over time, you are going to have to apply actions that reverse the damage.

Take responsibility - you have done this to yourself.

Taking corrective steps now will serve you in the long run because success is about playing the long term game. There are amazing returns for all those who are willing to endure the arduous journey of self-mastery.

The new healthy you, once again, will be more valuable to yourself and everyone you come into contact with especially your family and loved ones!

Chapter 22

LOVE AND HAPPINESS

Chase the Fairytale because it Exists

As I sit here typing this, it is the 13th of February 2019, the day before the official day of love, Valentine's day. I think it is fitting that I write this chapter today.

The woman in my life is asleep in the room, she seemed to have been rather tired today, and she called an early night. I just kissed her on the forehead and said goodnight, so I can come here and write this.

I've always respected the power of love. It is the only force that remains unexplained and yet the one that we gravitate towards no matter what happens. Love will sustain us regardless of how much we are hurt or disappointed by others.

It seems to continue to give people hope and is something people keep believing in. The subject of "love" had to make a feature in my book; not necessarily for advice but to share what I think are the critical and fundamental principles. I don't think I could have written this chapter if I had not met the woman I am with now.

In the past, I was attracted to more than my fair share of women. When I reflect on it now, I think women were attracted by my positive energy and my sense of mission. Sometimes I took advantage of this, and as a result, I hurt a few members of the opposite sex, and for that, I take full responsibility. I am sorry for poor past behaviour and for hearts that I hurt.

I am big enough to admit I treated some less than they deserved. I too, was hurt by some, and this is why I am compelled to address this subject. Love affects us all.

We all have hurt and have been hurt.

SELF-LOVE

People mention "self-love" all around the social media sphere with countless quotes being shared and reshared on platforms like Instagram. Take note on how many posts you see, and you will agree that it is an important topic. The feeling that says that you're ok and in harmony with yourself.

It is about being unapologetic about putting yourself first, not in a selfish way but in a way that calls you to take care of yourself, because you mean something.

This is where most people trip up and wonder why they end up in unpleasant situations. To love others, you need to love yourself first. If you don't value yourself, how can you value others?

The way you relate to yourself is how you end up relating to other people. The relationship you have with yourself sets the tone for the relationships you have with other people.

If you are a person that always puts other people first above yourself, the people you associate with will always put you second or lower in the rankings. What I am saying here is what I said before, you must first make it a priority to save yourself before you save others. Don't allow yourself to get caught up with the matters of everyone else while you suffer in silence battling with yours. Being selfish to a certain extent, with a healthy mix of selflessness will make sure you go pretty far, but you must learn to balance these.

RELATIONSHIPS

There are different types of relationships; but whether it be friends, emotional, family or business colleagues, the truth of the matter is that we cannot avoid entering into relationships.

Relationships are formed from the lightest associations; and they can grow into the most beautiful or the most destructive experiences. What these relationships become depends solely on the intentions both parties have towards each other.

There is a power that comes when you are able to actively set the tone for how people treat you in almost every relationship you form.

This is a result of defining who you are and unashamedly projecting what you will and will not tolerate from others.

Many go into the world wanting people to treat them a certain way. Yet, they fail to understand that every time they deal with a human being, they deal with a person who has their own feelings, thoughts, ideas, insecurities and intentions based on what they hold in high regard.

One has to exercise a lot of discretion when it comes to dealing with others. The basis of these relationships is formed from the relationship you have with yourself.

My relationships with people became more about me wanting them to unlock their potential, and as a result, I think I neglected my own vision in the process.

Sometimes I would feel that I wanted people to win first because I always felt that I could switch my magic on anytime and so I waited my turn. I didn't want people to hate me for shining. Because I put myself second, and because I was always the strong one who could handle a lot, everyone came to me for advice; nobody would ask me if I was ok. That bothered me until I made it a point to communicate to people that I too, indeed feel. This admission came as a shock to people. I decided that I was willing to let go of people that didn't get it; this was not an easy process.

This is how it will be for you the moment you decide to actively decide and set the tone for how you want to be treated. It all starts with you. You have to define the sort of treatment you expect from the people you associate with and stick to this regardless of how many people might be offended on your new standpoint.

Too many people expect to be treated a certain way, yet they don't project or communicate this to their world and then get disappointed when people don't read their minds.

With work projects, you find that you have to keep being on peoples cases to deliver on work and sometimes micro-managing is also required; we do this with work, but yet with other personal relationships we refuse to apply the same philosophy. Silence kills and that is something that took me a long time to learn. A closed mouth solves absolutely nothing!

If you want loving, and happy relationships with other people, you must accept that this doesn't happen by default or as some autonomous sequence of events; all relationships take effort. The best relationships are the ones that you've intentionally and actively invested in that compound over time.

You teach people how to treat you, and this starts by you once again assuming full responsibility and leaving nothing to chance. This is how happiness works too, misery is easy, and happiness takes constant asserted effort.

Happiness is not a destination or something someone gives you; happiness is a by-product and a state of mind that comes as a result of a person who lives intentionally in every aspect that life allows them to have control. Truly happy people don't make excuses.

GIVING AND RECEIVING

When it comes to giving and receiving love, I have seen that it all comes down to where you make investments.

You can only get something from something that you have invested in. The moment you come to terms with the fact that you cannot make withdrawals where you have not made deposits in this life; you learn not to expect too much from places you have not asserted yourself.

You reap what you sow, and this same logic applies to other people too. Don't allow people to make withdrawals in your life where they have not made deposits.

I'm also not saying everything should be measured and quantifiable because that would be absurd, but what I am saying is that you should be aware of where you stand with people. Consider how much they've invested in you, and adjust how much you expect from them accordingly and then do the same analysis from your perspective. This is not rocket science.

You will need to understand that love is not only about giving but also being able to receive. This took me a long time to understand because in general, we are more accustomed to understanding love from the perspective of giving than from the perspective of receiving.

It took the woman that I'm with to make me aware of this. My relationship with her has blossomed for nearly over a decade. It is unrehearsed natural care for each other that got us where we are, and I think a loving relationship at the right time is one of lifes' wonderful blessings.

This is not to say I have never loved before or been loved, but my relationship with her is the first of its kind for me. It is a ball of harmony and power. We are intentional about our relationship, and it happened to us when we weren't even looking for it. It also happened when our relationship with ourselves was of paramount importance.

Every time she looks at me. I see a person who loves everything about me and totally admires the man I've become. I am proud to present my best self to her and this assists in fueling me to improve on a daily basis.

I love her and everything she has become and who she is becoming. Naturally, we clash occasionally here and there, but we look out for each other. I am confident we will continue to do so as long as we live, because... it is a love that is real, and this makes it simple. You can't buy a caring heart towards you; she has taught me that it is ok for you to also receive as much love as you give.

It was Stephen Covey who spoke about the interdependent relationship that is comprised of two independent people who come together. This is a powerful relationship, and this type of relationship is miles apart from those where one party is a dependent person, and the other is an independent person; worse still is where you have two people together who are both dependent on each other.

I think that everyone should first chase themselves and become aware of themselves before they pursue relationships with other people. The more intact you are, the higher your standards and the more valuable you become to everyone you associate with.

Wisdom is there for anyone willing to ask the right questions to a better life.. Get yourself in order and be happy with yourself before you pursue others. This will save you a lot of unnecessary stress. You will not have to exaggerate and overcompensate who you are for what you lack; when you know who you are, you don't have to oversell yourself.

Love yourself and make your own subjective happiness a priority and be unapologetic about that. Know that you deserve to be loved and you deserve to be happy, so chase the fairytale because it exists; it just requires constant effort!

Chapter 23

CHARACTER

your Skills & Talents bring you into the Company of Kings, your Character will Keep you there.

"Be more concerned with your character than your reputation, because your character is what you really are, while your reputation is merely what others think you are."
- John Wooden

XXIII

I used to think life was all about achievements. I put a lot of emphasis on racking up impressive achievements, in hindsight, after years working on mastery of self, I have a different perspective.

Life is not only about achievements; it is about becoming a person of value and one of sound character. Be a person that others naturally want to have dealings with and want to be around.

Only when I cut out all of the unnecessary and destructive habits in my life, and really allowed the transformation to take place in me did I realise this.

Having character means that you are trustworthy, you gain the respect of others, you are responsible, fair, and you care about others. All leaders must be people of good character! Having poor character is the primary thing that removes people from positions of power.

Your skills and talents will bring you into the company of kings, but it is your character that will keep you there.

How many times have we heard of scandals, especially with celebrities, who then do all they can to do a PR clean up and deny all allegations simply because they are in the business of selling an image even though they struggle to live up to it?

In the world we live in today perception matters more than reality, and it's something that we've come to accept as a society. This is outright wrong! You can fabricate perception but beware - it is fleeting - then we wonder why we have such a rise in depression, anxiety and suicides globally.

You can build a good character - you cannot fabricate it.
You can fake it for a while, but the truth will always come out.

STAND FOR SOMETHING

You have got to have something that you stand for.

You have to have a set of standards, values and a code that you stand by. This code needs to be your unbreakable code.

There is an infinite number of options in this world that a person has access to; trying to experience them all is a fruitless endeavour.

Just because something is permissible does not mean it is all beneficial.
Just because something is legal does not mean it is right for you.

The sooner you can simplify your life and truly figure out who you are and what you want out of this life, the sooner you'll be able to enjoy your life. Clarity is power.

Once you simplify your life, you will be aware of the fact that you have more than enough time to do the things you want and need to do. Developing character helps prioritise things.

The fear of death is the reason people experience the so-called "mid-life crisis" because they feel that they don't have enough time left and so they become reckless with their choices.

When you are a person of character, your sense of self-awareness and your vision help impose the required self-discipline. This guided self-discipline lets you know which roads will get you there and which roads won't. It is for this reason that you're going to have to stand for something so you don't waste a lot of your precious time wandering in the desert.

The masses stand for nothing, and so they fall for anything. Life to them is about playing the game according to the crowd. Because the crowd does not have a set of values, anything goes.

An idle state of mind is a most dangerous thing; it will cause you to live by the dull default settings of life and not even be aware of it.

Your vision for your life must force you to set boundaries that you won't cross for the incubation of destiny. A person of character doesn't involve himself or herself in all things; they know exactly what they are here to do. Their commitment makes them unswayable.

YOUR LIFE IS IMPORTANT.

You must realise that your life is important. You are here for a reason, even though there will be times when you doubt this. You might have gone through some terrible things over the years; I'm here to tell you once again that you matter! There is a reason you are here;

there is something that needs to be accomplished, something that requires your input!

Your life has value so don't take it for granted or play with it. Life is not a pointless game. You must not go to the grave with your special work undone, because it is the work only you can do.

INTEGRITY

A person of character operates with integrity. This means that the things you say are the things you do.

Too many people are quick to make full vocal commitments only to follow through with less than half corresponding actions.

We have become a society that accepts broken promises and accepts half commitments. Society is ok with below-par standards.

I've often heard people say things like they always "leave room for disappointment."

Some enter important relationships like marriage because it is considered the next logical step and then live totally separate lives from the very commitments they've made.
Never do something based exclusively on the "wisdom" of the crowd, or just because it is "logical" - do it because it is right!
Make sure it is right for you and right of others involved.

Having integrity means that you are one, you are whole; there is no private life or public life; you have one life that you work on perfecting. This means getting your life in order by cutting out the things you are afraid of people finding out about and the vices that cannibalise your vision.

LOYALTY

When it comes to loyalty, I have seen that it is a quality that you can't expect to find in other people unless you demonstrate it first.

It is perhaps a good idea to prepare yourself for some disappointment when it comes to loyalty if you don't give it out. You might not receive it the first time you decide to be loyal but make a decision regardless to be a loyal person to everyone you expect it from, even if they betray you.

Eventually, loyal people will reveal themselves in your life.

Too many people claim to be loyal or were once loyal, only to get burnt by someone and then decide that they no longer will be loyal going forward. They then go forth after, and let everyone they come into contact with pay for the mistakes of those that wronged them. If you keep adding to the loop of disloyalty, how will you ever experience loyalty itself?

Loyalty and disloyalty become habits that eventually become automatic.

Make a decision to be a person that wants harmony in this life. You can either live in hell daily or live in heaven daily; the choice lies in your hands. The moment you take a stance, everything reflects back. It is not about expecting loyalty from people, but it is about you making the decision to be a loyal person to everyone you come into contact with and loyal to everything that you decide to start, regardless of whether they are loyal to you.

I am by no means saying you should be a pushover or a person who tolerates bad behaviour from others but what I am saying is that you make the decision not to participate in a negative way, just because everyone does.

The aim is for you to be better! I have been betrayed many times, by people I didn't expect to be betrayed by. In the beginning, I figured I had to deliver an eye for an eye, but over time I realised that there are more important things to this life and the people that betrayed me were stupid and short-sighted, and it would be something they forever would have to live with.

I wish them well, and all is forgiven, but they have lost access to me and my life and lost an extremely valuable and loyal individual.

Just because they betrayed me, I don't let that change who I am; instead, I go higher to a better place. I hold myself with extremely high regarding, and so I make sure I don't let my mind be occupied by feeble things most of the time, especially now that I understand the power of my thoughts and attention.

When you are betrayed, use the experience to evolve and to keep evolving, taking everything that hurts as a lesson that doesn't compromise who you are. This is power.

RESPONSIBILITY

In previous chapters, I strongly made the point of assuming full responsibility for your life. I will further extend on this now.

You are not going to only take full responsibility for your actions and your life, but you are also going to assume responsibility for everything you wish could change.

It is the things that make you angry or irritate you continuously that you were born to solve. You are not going to be a person who doesn't react to situations that bother you anymore and hope, they just go away. You are going to assume more responsibility and become a problem solver in the areas of this world you wish could be different. This means if there's a family situation that upsets you; instead of running from it, you are going to confront it head-on and deal with it in a positive, proactive way.

Let me extend this; if there is a cry in your circle of influence for something that once again irritates you that nobody wants to solve, you are going to assume the responsibility and put on your shoulders.

For example, if there's a constant financial problem in your circle of influence, you will solve the problem and also make sure you change the mindset that caused the problem. True responsibility demands you address the immediate need but then also dig down to the root of the problem and address that.

If there's a problem in your community that you feel should not exist, you are going to actively face it head-on and solve it.

You may not be able to immediately do this or always do this because you must first ensure you are strong enough within yourself.

But right now where you are, you will become aware of the things in your circle of influence that irritate you, and you are going to add this to your life to-do list regardless of when you will attend to them.

What I am proposing to you is going to give you a greater reason for living, and more energy. This will help you accelerate the process of becoming who you want to be. It is when there is a higher need that is greater than ourselves that we humans tend to rise to the occasion.

HELPING PEOPLE AND GIVING BACK

What I have said about character may be a tall ask, but you cannot gain the insights I have divulged in this book and only use them for yourself. Start with helping yourself and then you must help others.

The principles laid out in this book are to help you come into your own, to understand the fundamental reason why you are here. You are supposed to find your own promised land and then help those who are still stuck by living and expressing your divinity in a dark world that is starved of light. You are not here to hide away in the shadows and in the background, far away from people. You must allow yourself to make your presence felt in the world and to live loud and proud.

I also don't think there's anything gloried in becoming wise and then living up somewhere in the mountains away from society. I think there's tremendous power in withdrawing for some time, becoming powerful and coming back to dwell in the same world you left behind but now learn to work with it and lead it to a better future.

Become all that you can be and then go forth and help others become all they can be.

Open up doors for people and share in all that you have learnt because in that way you leave the world better than what you found it. That's what it's about.

Chapter 24

LAW OF DHARMA - PURPOSE

"Our greatest fear is not that we are inadequate. Our deepest fear is that we are powerful beyond measure. It is our light, not our darkness that most frightens us. We ask ourselves, Who am I to be brilliant, gorgeous, talented, fabulous? Actually, who are you not to be? Your playing small does not serve the world. We were born to make manifest the glory of God that is within us. And as we let our own light shine, we unconsciously give other people permission to do the same."
- Marianne Williamson:

XXIV

The Law of Dharma, which has had a changing meaning over time, is originally found in the ancient Sanskrit texts in Eastern Philosophy. The word "dharma" has a similar meaning to purpose in life, the law of nature as well as the Greek word "ethos" which refers to the character and ethical essence of the thing in question.

What drew me to the Law of Dharma was a question of "what I was here to do?" after I was in a car accident with my friends years ago. It would have been all over for me if we had gone over that bridge.

I remember asking myself: "What if I had to have died then? What would I have left behind? What was the evidence of my existence?"

It was then that I decided that I was going to do something that would last beyond my life. This led me to write the first two drafts of this book of which one I rejected, and the other was rejected by publishers.

I battled with understanding the reason behind my existence during my years at college/university. The question of my existence simply became larger and larger until I had to start allocating time to try to find the answers.

In hindsight, I don't think anyone needs a near-death experience to start to question their existence but what I know now is that the mere fact that you're asking yourself the question is a clear indication that you're already on the right track. Most people simply go through life daily without an awareness of themselves or their existence, and it is for this reason, I had to write this chapter.

ESSENCE OF THINGS

One of Aristotle's most beautiful philosophies was what he deemed "the essence of things" in which he asked the significance of why we assigned to the names to forms and processes we find in nature. Why do we call a bird a bird, why we call a snake a snake and a human being a human being? Also, why do we call the process of flight, flight? The essence of the things resides in the reason we call them the names we call them.

In my view, I see that nature does everything intentionally, and when you look at life, you can't help but marvel at the sheer magnitude of it; all the different programs that are running independently of you in such perfect harmony.

Sometimes I sit in awe of how everything fits into everything else. It is this that made me realise, that regardless of how insignificant I might feel in the grander scheme of things, there is a very crucial part I'm supposed to play in this vast existence; otherwise, I would've not appeared here.

This is the basis of truth: you have a role to play in life. There is a reason you are who you are, why you were born in this time, why you have been through the things you have been through, and why you can do the things you can do.

All this is true, even though you sometimes fail to recognise that. You have an essence about you, a full signature about you that makes up who you are and that lets people identify you amidst the billions of others that exist.

You are something that exists in a one of a kind form that will never exist again. There is a 1 in 400 trillion chance of you existing in this life and you being able to exist and read this is already a miracle in itself, and it's time you start accepting this.

You matter: this is a fact!

SELF-AWARENESS - ENDOWMENT

In the chapter about Vision, I touched on gifts, and I want to revisit this crucial aspect in the context of purpose.

Now that you understand that you are a one time deal, you are also going to have to realise that each one of us has latent talents and gifts. The way we express or deliver on these gifts or talents is unique to us. Many of us have been expressing or performing these gifts our whole lives without an awareness of this.

We are endowed with gifts, some more than others, some less. We have been drawn to places or events that perfectly relate to these gifts and talents in the world. This is why the timing of your existence is perfect.

Everything that is supposed to become something is already buried in itself. The egg has the chicken, and the seed holds the tree and even the forest within it. Nature shows us that the existence of something is supposed to go beyond what it currently is.

Everything has a higher form and evolution is mandatory. There can be no standing still in nature.

If something isn't busy growing, it is busy dying, but it cannot remain the same. You are here so that you can become more than what you are, and you will become this whether you are intentional about it or not (but being intentional about it will bring it to its best incarnation.) The seed must either germinate into a tree or die as a seed regardless of how slow or fast this process happens, but it cannot remain a seed forever. And this is true for all of us.

The greatest expression of who you are is already buried inside of you. Even though much of the material you will need to build will be found outside of you, never forget its origin and raw existence dwells within you. You have been doing it in lesser forms in its lowest expression without your awareness.

Success and life leave clues; the people who are closest to you have seen glimpses of this. This is why when you become successful people always say things like "but you always had that thing about you" or "I always knew you'd make it." What these people are talking about was an awareness of a constant expression of yourself even though it was minimal.

In school, when I was young, I was always the one who talked a lot! I was always disciplined for disrupting my classes and being told to keep quiet. It is now years later and speaking is now a big part of my career; I get paid to open my mouth now and what people deemed as a bother was actually a gift in disguise!

Ask yourself now what your unique gifts and talents are. This is a crucial part of the process of success, and regardless of how long this may take, you must discover your unique set of traits, talents or inclinations. Only when you have done this can you bring them centre stage for your purpose and inner transformation.

SELF-INVESTING

I once read a piece that spoke of how great work becomes great work. It basically said the more you work on something, the better it will become. There will be moments, particularly in the infancy stages, when it will feel that what you are trying to do sucks. This does not mean that it is insignificant.

For something to be great work, it usually will start off as being sucky work. This has been said before in this book - You must be a beginner at something in order to one day be a master at it, and this is why you never despise the day of small beginnings. When you see a person standing in front of thousands performing something, know that they probably practised that a thousand times when they were alone.

Your unique set of gifts and talents require you to not only identify them but also to invest in them. You must actively mould them into something greater than what they currently are. It is when you work on them that you get a feel of what you have and how great it can be.

This is where most fail; they invest in everything else but themselves because they don't think what they have is special or important, or they are too lazy to take it seriously. Your unique set of gifts, linked with your dreams, are your souls embedded escape plan from a dull world. Your art is your magic!

This is something you must make an active decision now to conquer. No longer can you live under the false pretence of assuming that your life will never amount to something. It is time to start taking yourself seriously because everything in you demands that you do so. The mere fact that you have bought this book and are on the second last chapter means that this passage is exactly for you and the mere fact that you found it means that you were looking for it. Because you are reading this book, you are already investing in yourself.

You must spend time on your unique set of talents and take yourself and them, seriously enough and invest the time, and whatever else they require for them to become something. This is something you're going to do regardless of how scared you might be or how useless you think it will be, you have to do it! Action is everything, and you can only reap where you sow.

You will start this process small with what you have where you are. A little here on the weekend and a little there the following week; this is a long term commitment.

SELF-MANIFESTATION - EXPRESSION

As soon as you start to work on your gifts and talents, you have to go out into the world and look for a way to express them.

This is much easier than before with the use of social media and the internet, but people must see you perform what you have, so you can know how good you are or how much you still need to improve on them.

This is where the fear of criticism stops people in their tracks! So many fear what people will say when they put themselves out there and you must expect judgement. Some will love what you have and others will hate it. You can't have one without the other. You must now start living beyond fear because as I said before, danger is real, but fear is just a false story you tell yourself.

You are going to put yourself out there while constantly refining who you are and what you have. This is the part where you must accept the feeling of standing out because a light was never meant to be hidden under the table, but it was meant to add light to the darkness.

It is for this reason that you have to manifest yourself into a world that is desperate for people who aren't held back by fear. When we put ourselves out there, we invite other people to do the same. You draw all beings who seek enlightenment through the process of you becoming and expressing yourself, and this is what your soul craves most apart from growth.

CONTRIBUTION

The last thing you are going to have to do with your unique set of talents after you have discovered, invested in, manifested and refined them into a formidable combination; is to use them to contribute to the needs and wants of humanity.

Remember that all existence (God, the Universe) seeks expression for us, through us and as us.

And when you use your endowments in order to serve others, you are fulfilling your highest purpose.

One small insignificant seed sprouts and grows, and the abundance of its fruits fulfils the needs of everything around it.

Your gifts and talents do not belong to you, and you only get to keep what you have by giving it away.

Your gifts and talents were freely given, their hard-earned fruits must now be given away, and when you do this, something special happens. This is when you unlock the ultimate secret to wealth. There are no limits to the number of people you can serve in the world with what you have when it is really powerful - this makes you irreplaceable.

Some will hate and despise you for doing this - I can tell you this from my research and personal experience. But know this: when people hate you for improving yourself, they don't hate you, they only hate themselves. Their reaction, while hurtful, must be of no concern to you, you are here for a higher mission. Do not be stopped by the screams of static people! People that are static are the most loud because motion in others confuses them. So take it all in your stride for this is part of the path to purpose!

Your purpose is not for you to find something deep to devote your life to, but to be all that you can be by the maximum expression of that which you have inside you so that you can serve as many people as possible.

This is the spiritual journey we signed up for that has brought us to this specific human experience.

CONSTANT LEARNING AND CONNECTION

The moment you understand the principles in this chapter, know that your life must constantly be committed to learning and improvement.

Because nobody can fire you from who you are, it means that there is no retirement in this for you because you are now going to be walking in the full magnitude of who you are, and this will continue until you breathe your last breath.

The more you know yourself, the more you work and perfect your unique offering, the more you will step into self-mastery.

With this self-mastery, you will be able to form new connections as you go that will allow you to create new things because of your own way of expression and perception of things.

You will gain a new powerful awareness of life that sets you apart, and people will be drawn to you from all over the world. Remain humble in your commitment to self-study.

Humility will ensure you remain mindful of your journey, remembering how difficult it was.

Remember that most people are struggling with this, accept their flaws and do not judge them for it. If people reach out to you for help, use your discretion wisely and know that it is not to use you but understand that in their darkness, they look to you as light.

Chapter 25

GRATITUDE AND COMPLETION - MASTERY

Go forth and step into your New life!

"Cultivate the habit of being grateful for every good thing that comes to you, and to give thanks continuously. And because all things have contributed to your advancement, you should include all things in your gratitude."
- Ralph Waldo Emerson

XXV

With all things that come your way going forward, be grateful for everything. Constantly give thanks for everything that has happened to you and be proud of your existence, love who you are through to the core and give care to the world around you remembering what you've had to endure.

You will carry yourself as a master knowing how the elements and the forces bend to your will and carry yourself with a calmness that surpasses all understanding. The world is now your oyster, and nothing is impossible for you, and there is nothing that you cannot be, do or have. You are powerful, and that power will affect and influence the world in a manner that you wish. My hope for you is that you will impart as much good as possible and impact as many people as possible.

I don't know where you find yourself right now, whether I still live or not, but I am proud of this book, and if I no longer exist, I am proud that my words live on and have found themselves to you.

Give thanks always! Never give up on the things that matter to you and that are close to your heart!

Go forth and step into your new life!

Enter Homo Magister; "Man the Master."

Poem by Edgar Albert Guest (1881 - 1959)

"Equipment"

"Figure it out for yourself, my lad,
You've all that the greatest of men have had;
Two arms, two hands, two legs, two eyes,
And a brain to use if you would be wise,
With this equipment they all began.
So start from the top and say, 'I can.'

Look them over, the wise and the great,
They take their food from a common plate,
And similar knives and forks they use,
With similar laces they tie their shoes,
The world considers them brave and smart,
But you've all they had when they made their start.

You can triumph and come to skill,
You can be great if only you will.
You're well equipped for what fight you choose;
You have arms and legs and a brain to use,
And the man who has risen great deeds to do,
Began his life with no more than you.

YOU are the handicap you must face,
You are the one who must choose your place.
You must say where you want to go,
How much you will study the truth you know;
God has equipped you for life, but He
Lets you decide what you want to be.

Courage must come from the soul within
The man must furnish the will to win.
So figure it out for yourself, my lad,
You were born with all that the great have had,
With your equipment they all began,
Get a hold of yourself and say: 'I CAN!'

BOOK RECOMMENDATIONS:

Start here...

"As a man thinketh" - James Allen
"Whatever you think, think the opposite" - Paul Arden
"The E-myth Revisited" - Michael Gerber
"The 10X Rule" - Grant Cardone
"The Alchemist" - Paulo Coelho
The Greatest Salesman in the World - Og Mandino

Intermediary:

"The 7 habits of Highly Effective People" - Stephen Covey
"Think and Grow Rich" - Napoleon Hill
"The 7 Spiritual Laws of Success" - Deepak Chopra
"Rich Dad Poor Dad" - Robert Kiyosaki
"The richest man in Babylon" - George S. Clason

Seasoned reader:

"The 48 laws of Power" - Robert Greene
"The Master Key system" - Charles F. Haanel
"Self Reliance" - Ralph Waldo Emerson
"Meditations" - Marcus Aurelius
"Outwitting the devil" - Napoleon Hill
"The Science of getting rich" - Wallace D. Wattles

WHERE TO FIND ME:

WEBSITE

www.tmcglobal.co

INSTAGRAM

@masterlui_

FACEBOOK

facebook.com/TMCGlobalEdu

SPEAKING

Book me to speak at your conference.
info@tmcglobal.co

Made in the USA
Middletown, DE
22 September 2020